SURVIVING THE HUMAN JUNGLE

HOW ONE GIRL CONQUERED HER MANY LIFE TRAUMAS TO FLOURISH

Annie Dism

SURVIVING THE HUMAN JUNGLE

Annie Dism

Surviving the Human Jungle

Published by Spines

ISBN: 979-8-89383-301-0

In memory of my aunt, my angel.

Chapter 1

She awoke from her nap on her parents' bed in a room in the center of the silent, small, wood-frame house. Her immediate thought was to call for her mom, which she did. She heard nothing in return. Becoming concerned by the absence of response and complete silence in the house, she called again and again – nothing. The small three-year-old girl cautiously stepped onto the floor and bravely walked into the doorway of the kitchen as she began to cry in fear of being alone. Her eyes searched the room as she called for her mom again but saw no one and heard nothing. As the small girl continued to cry, she built up the courage to walk farther into the kitchen to peer into the living room. She still saw no one. Still crying and calling for her mom without response, the young child gained enough courage to walk onto the screened porch and peer outside where the automobiles were always parked. Knowing her dad had taken one automobile to work far away for the week, the child looked for the other. It was not there. There were no automobiles there. She then knew she was home alone and began crying hysterically. She quickly ran back into the house, into her parents' bedroom, and climbed back onto their bed. She continued to cry as she wondered how long it would take for her extended family to find her alone and take her home with them. She thought of the possibility of it taking two to three days. That small, three-year-old girl, Sidonie, immediately believed that her mom had abandoned her.

A short time later, which seemed like much longer to that little girl, her mom returned home to find her young daughter crying hysterically for being left alone. Her mom asked what was wrong, as if she did not know. She was well aware of her daughter's fear of being alone, even if she was only alone inside the home with her parents just outside. Her mom explained that she had gone to Sidonie's grandparents' home to wash laundry and insisted she was only gone for a few minutes. The grandparents' home was three houses from their home with two small pastures between the other homes. Her mom quickly became frustrated with Sidonie for continuing to cry and began to scold her for overreacting because she had not gone far from the home, was not gone for long, and the child was asleep when she left. She expected her to still be asleep when she returned. She seemed to feel the need to defend herself, refusing to consider she had done anything wrong by leaving her three-year-old child home alone.

The small girl's intense fear of abandonment is a strong indication that her mom, within those prior three years, had treated her in a manner that caused her to believe that her mom did not want her. Not remembering the first three years did not mean Sidonie was not affected by the trauma of them. She definitely was. That was the first of two memories retained from that age by Sidonie as she grew older. That feeling of not being wanted by her mom remained as it continued to be confirmed by the way she was treated. There were a couple of other incidents during Sidonie's early childhood in which she believed her mom may have abandoned her.

The mom of this child was twenty years of age at this time. She had become a wife and mom of a son at the age of fourteen, while still a child herself. Because of her adult responsibilities, she had not had the opportunity to finish developing and maturing psychologically as most teenagers; therefore, there was much she had not learned and did not understand to be successful in those adult roles with those adult responsibilities. She still needed parenting but no longer had that. In addition, she had repeatedly witnessed physical abuse within her childhood home. She entered into motherhood with issues from that trauma.

Sidonie's second memory that she retained as she grew older also occurred at the age of three. She was very close with her dad even though he was not around much. He loved and adored her. He was always expressing his love for her with affection. He would also defend her to her mom and protect her from her mom's discipline. He was very loving toward his baby girl, but not his wife or son. With a smile, that father instructed his three-year-old daughter to say derogatory words to her mom. This had probably been occurring prior to this first memory of this behavior, as it felt normal to this young toddler who had no understanding of the words which she was repeating nor the meaning of what she was saying. Her mom immediately became upset and angry, but more toward her small child than her husband. Her mom scolded her and threatened her with discipline should she continue to repeat her dad's words, but as always, her dad scolded Sidonie's mom and warned her that she was not to do anything to Sidonie.

Sidonie did not understand what she was doing

wrong as she was rewarded with playful affection and laughter from her dad. She was making her dad happy. She was confused in this battle between her parents of which she was somehow in the middle. The happier she made her dad, the more she upset her mom. This type of situation recurred repeatedly into the age of four and possibly five, until Sidonie's comprehension developed enough to understand that it was hurtful to her mom and wrong. She then refused to grant her father's wishes each time. Eventually, her father no longer attempted to initiate such behavior. However, Sidonie's mom seemed to resent her.

This mom feared her husband because he physically abused her. She had left a home in which she witnessed the physical abuse of her mom and brother to unsuspectingly enter a home in which she was directly abused physically and psychologically. Her husband had also grown up in a home of physical abuse, as well as psychological abuse, although he did not only witness that abuse. He also experienced it directly. The abuse from his father was severe and even brutal at times. This created serious issues for her husband, including anger issues. He had not had anyone to help him deal with his issues from the trauma of the abuse because no one who was aware of the abuse knew how to deal with it themselves. All the negative emotions turned into anger which was released onto his wife and son.

The young, innocent girl began retaining many more memories after turning four years old. It was at that tender age that she was approached by an older boy, who was regularly a part of her life, about something unknown and strange to her. He explained that he had been informed by a boy a little older than him about something adults did but did not want children to do. In his curiosity, he wanted to experiment with her, but she could not tell anyone. Sidonie had been taught by her parents that anyone older than her in her life knew more than her regarding what she was allowed and not allowed to do. Her understanding was to trust them for such things when adults were not around. She assumed that what the boy was referring to was probably something adults preferred children to not do, but not necessarily wrong. Sidonie had no idea the situation she was getting into. It was uncomfortable, awkward, and felt wrong, but she did not know how very wrong it was. If it were very wrong, that boy would not have chosen to do such a thing. Regardless, Sidonie did not want to get the boy in trouble afterward for what he had already done. Although older, he was still a young child also. The boy who had told him about this activity, although older, was also a child who was told by an older child, who was told by a young teenager.

Such incidents occurred a few more times within a few years. Each time, Sidonie was a little older and more mentally developed, and each time it felt like a more serious wrong. As she began to understand how wrong that activity was and that she should refuse to cooperate, the boy completely quit attempting to engage with her in that type of activity. Sadly, this was not the last of such a situation for Sidonie. Throughout all of this, the physical and psychological abuse within Sidonie's home continued.

Sidonie awoke one Saturday morning and ran into the living room to watch cartoons. As she entered the living room, she saw a woman who was married to her mom's cousin sitting in the recliner. The woman was close with Sidonie's family and Sidonie adored her. Curious as to why she was there that early in the morning, Sidonie walked to the chair and climbed onto the woman's lap. Her mom was sitting in a chair to the left, and her dad was sitting on the sofa to the right. Reading the curiosity on Sidonie's face, her mom explained that the woman's husband had physically abused her the night before, so she slept at their home. She felt bad for the woman. Then, something seemed strange to Sidonie. It was something strange between the woman and her dad. She looked at the woman's face, then her dad's face, back at the woman's face, then her dad's face again. She felt very strong, uncomfortable vibes between them. Even though the woman and her dad were not looking at each other, the five-year-old girl knew that the two were having inappropriate relations. The woman chose to return to her home later that day. This affair was confirmed to Sidonie in her early adult years by someone who had known of the affair.

The horrible emotions Sidonie felt with each incident of abuse within her home cannot be accurately described. Watching her brother being lashed on occasion with a belt or other item with such force to leave bruises emotionally scarred Sidonie. The fear of watching her mom being beaten and the terror that she would be killed during those moments was completely devastating. However, she had always felt she, herself, safe with and protected by her father, as he had never done anything to indicate even a remote possibility of harming Sidonie. There were times as Sidonie grew older that she wished she were the target of the abuse instead of her mom and brother. She once attempted to take the blame for something her brother did in an effort to protect him from the abusive consequences. Her father would not have it. She would hear the awful demeaning and degrading things her father would say to and in front of her mom and brother about each of them. That severely disturbed her as she understood how it must have made them feel, even though those things said were not true. She also realized as she got older that her brother actually believed some of those things their dad said about him to be true. It was represented in his behavior.

The last time her dad beat her mom, her mom instructed her eight-year-old son to go fetch his aunt next door. He ran out of the house as quickly as possible. As he ran hastily across the yard, his angry dad in his violent rage yelled through the window threatening harm to his son if he reported the event. His son did not stop running in an effort to rescue his mom. The dad returned to beating his wife. Then six years old, Sidonie attempted to stop her dad from beating her mom by grabbing his arm. His facial expression, tone of voice, and cold eyes as he threatened his very young daughter that she “better back off” frightened her in a way she had never experienced. She felt the threat of physical harm to her.

After intervention stopped her dad from further beating her mom, her mom called her family. Upon their arrival, Sidonie was taken into the car with her two aunts. As they were preparing to leave, Sidonie’s dad went to the car wanting to tell his daughter goodbye. She did not want to open the window. His eyes were teary with a trace of red expressing emotional pain. He was upset that they were leaving, especially his baby girl. One of Sidonie's aunts encouraged her to open the window to tell her dad goodbye. She hesitantly and with fear did so with a kiss, then quickly retracted from him. She feared what he might do to her if she did not kiss him goodbye as he requested. From that day forward she was no longer able to completely trust her dad for her safety and protection. She already had the fear of abandonment from her mom, and now she had the fear of physical harm from her father. They lived with Sidonie's maternal family for two weeks.

After those two weeks, Sidonie's mom decided to return home and give her husband another chance on a trial basis. They did not move all their belongings with them during this trial period. They had only returned approximately two weeks when one calm, starry night, the sleepy young girl lay her head on her mom's lap as she drove them home from a visit with her grandparents. As they traveled through the last curves of the road before reaching their home, Sidonie noticed the sky was unusually bright for a night sky. As they rounded the last curve, the sky became brighter. She sat up to see more and attempted to determine the cause. As they got closer to their home, Sidonie began to recognize the light as flames. Then, she realized the flames were above her home.

As they arrived, Sidonie saw the flames raging from her home. She exited the automobile with her mom and learned that her dad had also just arrived. No one had been home to know what caused the fire or make any attempt to extinguish it before it spread. Not knowing how to deal with losing her home and all her belongings inside, Sidonie cried for her baby doll. That was the only way she knew to express such loss. After hearing that sad cry from his baby girl, her father entered the home in an attempt to retrieve her baby doll and possibly a few other items, but the situation quickly became too dangerous. Discouraged and saddened by his failure to make the situation a little easier for his daughter, he had to exit the home for his own safety. He did not realize that it was not losing her doll that upset her so. It was the sadness of the loss of her home.

Sidonie was not there for long when a neighboring family member brought her to her nearby grandparents' home. Their family living next door did not know the house had caught fire until it was beyond individual control. Living far from the nearest fire station, Sidonie's home and all her belongings burned completely. Within that year, they built a new home.

The abuse continued, except that her father never again actually hit her mom.

Usually, the only wrongs Sidonie did were what her brother and the other boys did so that they would not exclude her, not wanting to play with her anymore. The children she had in her life were mostly boys who were also cousins of varying distances. It was not often that other girls were around besides her much older cousins. She did not often do the wrongs which the boys did. She had her limits of how wrong she would do and even that did not occur often. While the new house was being built, Sidonie was challenged by her brother to jump from the floor of the second story to the ground as he had done. Being afraid of heights, she hesitated, contemplated, then finally convinced herself to jump. She knew her parents would not approve of her jumping from that distance, but she thought it was not necessarily wrong and not dangerous after watching her brother land safely. It did not occur that way for Sidonie. Upon landing, her face hit the ground. She stood up and seemed fine until her brother saw blood coming from the edge of her face and realized it was cut. He informed her of the injury and that it was not minor. It would need more than a bandage.

Since preparing the property to build the house, they had all been finding glass bottles in the soil with some of them broken. Her brother guided her to the front of the house out of their parents' view to discuss what story to tell their parents regarding how her face was cut. It was normal for Sidonie, her brother, and their mother to alter or create new explanations for occurrences. The children learned to do this from their mother. It was done to protect them from the harsh consequences of Sidonie's dad. It was survival instinct. It is very sad that the mother had to teach her children to lie to anyone, especially their father. It was even sadder that she had to do it for their protection as well as her own.

They told their parents that they were running around the house and Sidonie fell, probably landing on a piece of glass. Their parents believed their story because the cut was smooth, not jagged. Considering the smoothness of the cut as stated by their parents, the children determined among each other that it was very possible Sidonie's face was cut by glass when she landed. Their story was probably not a complete lie. They did not notice glass on the ground where she landed at the time she stood up, but they did not look at that moment. Her parents knew her face needed to be stitched but did not want to take her to the hospital. They never had health insurance and did not want the out-of-pocket expense. Her parents discussed the situation. Then, her mom called one of

Sidonie's aunts and asked her to stitch Sidonie's face. Her aunt had no medical education or experience. She was older than Sidonie's parents and their most knowledgeable family member, but not in medical procedures. Sidonie's aunt and her husband arrived at their temporary home while their new one was being built. Fortunately for Sidonie, her aunt and uncle went to their home to convince her parents to take Sidonie to the hospital for medical treatment. They were both much smarter with more knowledge and wisdom than Sidonie's parents and knew it would be dangerous for any one of them to perform the stitching. Sidonie's parents initially resisted and persisted in convincing her aunt to perform the procedure. They finally agreed to take Sidonie to the hospital. The doctor performed the stitching on her face, and she recovered fine. There were other incidents in which Sidonie's extended family were of assistance in situations that could have resulted in bad outcomes had they not persuasively intervened. If her extended family had been involved more, Sidonie's childhood would have probably been significantly better. Her large number of extended family members each played a crucial role in Sidonie's life. She was very close with them. She learned much from them and some of them really knew her. They listened to her to be able to know her. They are probably the reason she survived her childhood and grew into the adult she became.

As Sidonie grew out of her toddler years, her mom began repeatedly telling her she was spoiled, mean, hateful, selfish, lazy, slow, stupid, and had no common sense. Those things were not all told to her at the same time, but often. She would also sometimes ask Sidonie what was wrong with her, and other times tell her something was wrong with her. She even specifically insisted to Sidonie there was something mentally wrong with her. All these things were always said in a harsh, degrading tone. Sidonie began analyzing herself and her behaviors and analyzing others for comparison. She was determined to recognize the bad in herself and understand why her choices and behavior were wrong so that she could correct it all and be good and normal.

Sidonie and her brother were playing outside of their new home one afternoon when their much older first cousin arrived on his bike. He was a young adult, and the children were very close with him. He was like an older brother. He wanted to run along the beach in front of their home. The children went with him. Upon returning, their mom met them outside. She was very angry with them because they had not told her where they were going, and she did not know where they were. This was unusual because the children had been out of sight for longer periods without their mom being so angry. It was common and even encouraged for children to play outside without the confinement of close proximity of the home. She scolded Sidonie and her brother then sent them inside to take their baths. She said that it was her turn to go run with their cousin. The children found that strange. She had never done anything like that before and something seemed strange with both of them. The cousin was their dad's biological nephew, their mom's nephew by marriage. While Sidonie's brother was preparing her bath, he told her he was going to look for their mom and cousin. He did so while Sidonie bathed. Upon his return, he explained to her as best he could, without getting graphic, what he had seen. He saw the two engaging inappropriately. They were having an affair. By then, the children knew their dad was commonly unfaithful to their mother and not only with ongoing affairs. It was very disappointing to learn their mom was also unfaithful, especially unfaithful with her nephew, even if the relation between them was not biological.

A much older family member confirmed this affair as Sidonie was approaching her adult years. Her family always thought she did not know what occurred with her own immediate family members, but she did, even if only by intuition. What she did not know was that her brother had told their father what he had seen. That knowledge explained the long period of very bad, daily treatment their dad had inflicted upon their mom after that incident, eventually leading to their mom leaving their dad for a couple of weeks. It also explained her brother's loss of respect for their mom which eventually led to him becoming combative with her once.

One evening sometime later, Sidonie's uncle, who was her mom's brother, and his wife arrived at their home. Almost immediately after their arrival, Sidonie and her brother were sent to watch television in their parents' bedroom while their parents, uncle, and aunt watched a movie inappropriate for children on the device in the living room. That was not abnormal. Their parents were appropriately strict about the content their very young children watched. Their parents' behavior on this particular evening was not quite so normal. Both children were suspicious. Their parents stressed to Sidonie and her brother that they were not to go downstairs for any reason. As the children watched television, Sidonie's brother decided to change the channel to that on which the device in that bedroom played. Those devices were not connected to one another in any way. What was watched on one, could not be seen on the other. The film had to be inserted into that specific device to watch that specific film. Very strangely and still unknown how, the content being played in the living room was transmitting to the device in the bedroom. It was pornography. They checked that device and determined that was definitely not what was on the film inside. Sidonie was very disturbed by what she was seeing while her brother seemed interested. She insisted he change the channel. He did, only to return to that channel a few minutes later. He attempted to convince her to watch, but she again insisted a few times that he change it, and he did. Sidonie could not understand why anyone would do such things for others to watch. She thought that should be very personal and private. She also could not understand why anyone would want to watch such things. Most disturbing to her was that her mom was watching pornography with her own brother. In addition, her dad was watching pornography with someone else's wife. Those circumstances felt very wrong and completely inappropriate to Sidonie.

Sometime after the inappropriate incidents with the older boy ceased but when Sidonie was still very young, an older girl became a part of Sidonie's life. The older girl wanted to have a pretend wedding in which the two of them were getting married. From there, the older girl led Sidonie to something more. Being a little older with a better understanding, she briefly considered the possibility of what the older girl was wanting to do, but she quickly dismissed that possibility because she did not think that any such thing could occur between girls. Sadly, Sidonie realized she was wrong after it had gone too far. Still being very young, she did not know how to end that situation at that point.

In the second attempt by the older girl, Sidonie immediately realized what the older girl wanted to do. Sidonie told the older girl that she did not want to do that. The response was that she would tell Sidonie's mom if she did not do it. Sidonie knew that meant the older girl would tell Sidonie's mom what Sidonie had already done with her. Still feeling that her mom did not really want her, Sidonie believed her mom would blame her, truly hate her, and either abandon her or treat her even worse than she already had been. Because of that fear, Sidonie hesitantly co-operated. Sidonie became disgusted with the older girl and began attempting to exclude her from her life, but the older girl was very persistent and put Sidonie in situations in which she could not refuse having her around without some explanation as to why. There were a few more such incidents with that older girl before she moved.

Sidonie was relieved when the older girl moved from the area. She believed there would be no more opportunities for her to do that to Sidonie. Much to her surprise, she was in the presence of that older girl again a few months later at another location. The older girl wanted Sidonie to go to her and sit on her lap. Sidonie, with her head down in emotional discomfort, did not move from her mom's side, which confused her mom as well as the older girl's family members. At the encouragement of them all, Sidonie hesitantly walked to the older girl and sat on her lap. She was very uncomfortable as she was afraid the older girl would somehow manage to guide her to another room without suspicion of the others to repeat those unwanted actions. She had hoped to never see that girl again, and now she was with her and at risk of what she thought she had finally escaped. Much to her relief, that was the extent of what occurred during that visit, and that was the last time she saw that girl.

Throughout her early childhood, there continued to be attempts at such activity by young boys. Sidonie was with her parents at their friends playing outside with the other children there. The mother of that home did not allow children in the house while adults were visiting. The children always had to play outside, and Sidonie's parents did not dispute that. While playing outside, the boy who lived at that home and the neighbor boy attempted to convince Sidonie to enter the doghouse with the neighbor boy, who had already entered first. As she began to enter, she felt that something was wrong. Their facial expressions and the look in their eyes made her uncomfortable. She then suspected that they were going to attempt something inappropriate with her, so she backed out and went away from that area. She later learned that the neighbor boy's father would watch pornography in his home on satellite television and the boy would often discreetly watch unseen by his parents. She was then sure that was why he wanted her in the doghouse with him, and the other boy was assisting him to accomplish that.

There were incidents at other times at that same home of boys attempting to touch Sidonie's private area. She ran from them as they chased her with determination until they finally accepted that they would not catch her. Then, she would maintain a distance from them, so they could not surprise her. She considered telling the adults, but anytime the children entered the house, the mother of that home would send them back out without allowing them to say what they needed. Fortunately, Sidonie understood more, knew better, and was able to prevent inappropriate activity with her from ever occurring again during her childhood. However, she witnessed such activity of other children a few times, which was disturbing to her. It seemed normal to those other children, but it never felt that way to her. She was not curious about adult activities. She was comfortable with the things that were for children and leaving the rest for adults. She was not eager to be an adult by doing adult things. Perhaps she wanted to have what little of a childhood she could.

As Sidonie's older brother was approaching his teen years, he also began saying degrading things to her in demeaning tones. It was a learned behavior from their mom, he now resented her also. Their parents had always been very biased toward their children. Her dad was very partial to her and harshly mean to her brother. Her mom was very partial to her brother and mean to her. Now her brother began engaging with their mom against Sidonie. Sometimes, her mom and brother would join each other in ridiculing and patronizing her in degrading manners. They also regularly accused her of having ill intentions in many situations in which they were wrong. She generally did not cause trouble, was rarely disobedient, did not like anyone being physically or emotionally harmed, and did not act out at any age. Her brother was more that type, although Sidonie seemed to be the only one aware of that. She knew most of what he did as she was usually with him to witness. She relentlessly attempted to be good and do right, but they assumed the opposite of her. Sidonie did not want to make things worse than they already were by creating more problems, except when her brother tormented her. He loved to tease her in mean manners to provoke a reaction from her. She would tell her mom who would do nothing. He would continue until she could tolerate no more. She would eventually react in the only way that was effective. She would attack him. Initially, he would laugh in amusement until it became painful. Then, he would get angry but knew the consequences from his dad if he were to physically react to her, so he did not and would finally quit teasing her. Her mom scolded and disciplined Sidonie for doing what she could to stop her brother's psychological torment when her mom should have stopped it. She never scolded or disciplined her son for what he did to Sidonie. On occasion, Sidonie would tell her dad of such incidents when he would return home, but only when they became excessive and intolerable for Sidonie. She hated getting her brother in trouble with her dad, but sometimes that was the only way to stop him from tormenting her regularly and often since her mom would not stop him.

Sidonie knew she was different. It was obvious and her mom regularly made her aware. She believed that if she was different from both of her parents and her brother, she had to be different from everyone else also. All three could not be the ones who were different and she be the only normal one, so it was easy for Sidonie to believe there was something wrong with her. She believed she would always be an outcast if she did not correct what was wrong with her. Sidonie truly felt that she did not belong anywhere with anyone. It was an awfully lonely feeling. She felt very insignificant.

The psychological abuse of Sidonie by her mom did not occur in the presence of others and continued throughout her childhood and beyond. Her dad was not around much throughout her childhood, so it was easy to hide it from him. He either worked all day during the week or worked far away and gone all week only to be home on the weekends. When he was not working, he seemed to always have other priorities and was gone much of the day. Sometimes, he was also gone in the evenings until late. He seldom allowed any of them to go with him.

When Sidonie's dad was home, there was no way to know when his anger would explode into rage. Sometimes, he would be happy then suddenly get angry and mean. There was no way to know what might provoke him because things that did not bother him at a prior time might provoke him in that present moment. Also, things that had provoked him at a prior time might not bother him in that present moment. Sidonie, her brother, and their mom lived every day of their lives with great tension, even when her dad was not there. They never knew what his mood would be when he returned home. The tension in their home was always very strong, remaining with them to some degree everywhere they went.

It was not all bad for Sidonie. She had good memories with each of them. Her mom would sometimes play games with her, color with her, dance with her, and chase her around the house to tickle her. She was affectionate with both her children. Her brother was sometimes a great brother. They played together, he taught her things, and he was protective of her with others who had ill intentions toward her. He and their mom could treat her badly, but he would not allow anyone else to do so. Sidonie's dad had always been loving toward her when not angry. He also enjoyed spoiling her in the ways that he could. Although, as she began to understand the difference of the treatment of her compared to that of her brother and mom, she attempted to minimize her father's partial treatment of her to minimize the emotional pain it caused her bother and mom. She understood how hurtful it was for them to see how capable he was of giving love but refused to give any to them.

Holidays were wonderful for Sidonie. They gathered with their entire extended paternal family for the whole day, and for two consecutive days for some holidays. She absolutely loved spending time with all of them. There was much love and care between them all. They were always there for each other, and she felt some belonging with them. All Sidonie's security was with them. Those were her best and favorite times. They were the highlights of her childhood and beyond.

Sidonie had many times wanted to tell adults within her extended family what was occurring within her home and how they were being treated, but sharing such information with anyone was not as option. Her large extended family were all as close as immediate family. Everyone's business was shared throughout the family, except for some of the abuse within individual homes. Although her family knew of some of the abuse, there was much they did not know, including the abuse of children in some of the homes. Sidonie should have been able to seek help from some of her family members, but everything that was shared regarding what occurred in her home was eventually shared with her parents. The consequences of sharing information about the mildest of mistreatment unseen by others indicated how much worse it would have been had she shared more. Her extended family members did not have ill intentions when informing her parents that Sidonie had shared such information. They would inquire about those incidents out of concern, unsure that Sidonie was telling the accurate truth. Children were not trusted to voice things accurately and in the correct context. They expected children to have misconceptions. Sidonie's parents would always minimize the situations when confronted by other adults, and that was believed to be the accurate truth. There was no point in telling any other adult because the outcome would have been the same, and the consequences would have been too much for her to endure.

Before Sidonie reached her teen years, she went with her parents to the home of her uncle and aunt. They had recently purchased a television satellite dish. This was still a new concept with many more channels to watch than anyone had previously had access to. Most of her dad's family gathered there to watch television. Sidonie was instructed to sit at the kitchen bar with her mom, their backs to the television. All of her aunts joined them in the kitchen while her uncles and adult male cousins gathered around the television in the living room with some of her cousins' wives. There was nothing separating the living room and kitchen. It was completely open. They set the volume too low to hear and Sidonie's mom instructed her to not look in the direction of the television. She was to only look into the kitchen. Sidonie never attempted a glimpse, especially when she realized what they were watching. Nothing inappropriate was said, but she could tell by their mannerisms and things that were said, they were watching pornography. Again, Sidonie was disturbed. She had no desire to see any of it. She was not at all curious. It was disgusting to her. After a while, Sidonie was sent to a bedroom and was not allowed to come out until her parents were ready to leave. The most disturbing was the fact that these men and women were watching pornography together; men with their brother's wives, nephew's wives, and son's wives, and cousins with their cousin's wives, their aunts, and their mothers. Sidonie could not understand how any of them could possibly not be extremely uncomfortable. She also could not understand people's interest in watching others engage in acts which were so personal and private, especially watching that with others who were not even a significant other, then family! It was sickening to her.

Chapter 2

During her teen years and possibly prior, when Sidonie attempted to share her opinions, thoughts, or feelings with her mom, her mom would scold her for having the wrong opinions, thoughts, or feelings then, tell her what they were to be without any explanation or perspective for her to understand and learn. She simply wanted Sidonnie to be exactly as she wanted and was told to be by her without ever thinking for herself. She never seemed to like the person Sidonie was. This occurred with the inclusion of degrading words, so she quit sharing those things which were a significant part of the individual person she was. This made her feel dismissed as unimportant and insignificant. She hated feeling like she never mattered to the ones who she was supposed to matter to most. Her mom could not know her child without knowing her thoughts and perception of matters. She did not seem to want to know her. She instead wanted to make her into who she wanted her daughter to be.

As Sidonie approached her teens, she blocked the memories of her childhood molestation. That young child within seemed to fade away, and a new soul emerged into the same body. Perhaps those memories had left with that young child. This new person had the innocence that had been taken from that young child through the sexual abuse. The teenage years were very difficult for Sidonie. While struggling with her self-esteem and self-worth, her parents became very strict with her. Additionally, she was very sheltered. She often wondered why she ever existed. No one's life would have been any different if she had not, unless better. She felt that she was a nuisance to her family and possibly everyone else as well. She believed everyone's life would probably be better had she never existed.

When Sidonie's brother was sixteen, an argument ensued between her parents while she and her brother were outside on the porch. It escalated and became very intense. The door was open, and the children could see everything. Their mother was in the corner of the room against the wall with their dad standing in front of her. Their dad's fist was up and pulled back ready to strike a punch. Sidonie begged her brother to intervene, but he did not. This continued for a few minutes as the intense argument continued with their dad's abusive words to their mother. Sidonie could not endure her mom being hit again and after all these years. She hated her dad at that moment.

Eventually, the situation deescalated without their dad hitting their mom. Sidonie could not understand why her brother, at his current age, would not attempt to intervene to prevent their dad from hitting their mom again after all those years. Perhaps he still feared their dad to that extent even though their dad was no longer physically abusing her brother. Perhaps he believed their mom deserved it for her affair years prior. That was a common perception among many of their family members. It was much worse for a woman to be unfaithful than a man. For some reason, a man's unfaithfulness was much more accepted and a woman deserved abuse for her unfaithfulness. Fortunately, Sidonie's brother did not become a physical abuser as many who grow up with that example.

Sidonie continue to feel like she did not belong throughout her childhood and a couple of years beyond. She knew she was different from her parents and her brother. Her mom convinced her that she was different from everyone. Her mom harshly declared her too sensitive when she got upset for feeling someone was mistreated, especially when Sidonie felt she was the one mistreated. Her dad sometimes scolded her for those things, but in a different way. He did not scold her harshly. Her dad would get upset because Sidonie was upset. He wanted his little girl to be happy. He disliked seeing her heartbroken. Her dad appreciated his daughter's caring nature but did not know how to deal with it because that nature had not been allowed in his childhood home. He mildly scolded Sidonie with an explanation about the situation in an effort to remove her sadness. He was not trying to scold her. His tone was usually harsh in most situations, which was the result of his upbringing resulting in anger and misery.

During her early childhood, Sidonie was constantly caught between her mom and brother and her dad, even when her dad was not around. During her teen years, she felt invisible. Her parents were very strict. She was not allowed to leave the house much, but her family seemed happier when she was quietly in the background. Her mom and brother were not interested in her. Her dad did not know how to relate to her during that time. They simply wanted her there under their complete control. She was mostly ignored, so Sidonie spent most of her time alone in her room.

She made a new friend upon entering middle school. Their mothers were distant family to each other and had always known each other, so Sidonie was allowed to spend much time with her new friend and her family. The two girls quickly became best friends and Sidonie eventually became like a part of her friend's family. One day while Sidonie was spending the weekend with them, an argument ensued between her friend's mother and stepfather as the girls were watching television. The mother and stepfather were in the kitchen, but Sidonie could see everything occurring. As the argument escalated, Sidonie became nervous. Then, she observed the two step closer to each other. Their faces were very close as the argument escalated more. Sidonie became afraid upon that observation. She was sure the man would hit his wife. She looked at her friend who seemed to have no concern as she continued watching television. Sidonie looked at the adults again, then back at her friend. She asked her friend if she was not worried. Her friend replied that she was not. She explained to Sidonie that the argument would end soon, and everything would be normal between the two again. That explanation confused Sidonie with all that she was observing. Much to her surprise, her friend was correct. Soon after, the argument ended, and the mother and stepfather were as they normally were with respect and consideration for each other. There had been no abuse, physical or psychological. That is when

Sidonie realized that abuse between husband and wife was not normal. It was not necessary and should not occur. She was fortunate to have had that experience and gain that knowledge. Some of her family members had not been as fortunate. They thought the abuse was normal and occurred in all marriages as they entered marriages in which they became physically abused for years before finally removing themselves from those situations.

Sidonie's middle school years were confusing. She felt lost. She was attempting to belong somewhere. She had quickly made new friends, but they knew nothing of the truth of her life. She and a childhood friend who lived nearby had grown apart some. He was an only child. Those two had been almost like brother and sister. They seemed to grow farther apart after he entered high school, which was two years before she entered. He acknowledged her at school, but not much more than that. He once spoke to her when she was near, so she went stand closer to him to socialize with him more. His friends ignored her. He and his friends barely spoke at all, even between each other. It was clear his friends did not want her around and he did nothing to change that. He was busy with his own social life while trying to find his way in the world and made no effort to include Sidonie. That hurt, but she never allowed it to be known to anyone. She felt abandoned by him as well as her brother. She felt that she had no one on the level that she needed. She had no one who knew the truth about her life at home or who she could trust to confide in to be there for her in the way she desperately needed.

The very day before beginning her first day of high school, her brother, who was beginning his last year there, very adamantly insisted Sidonie not tell anyone at school that she was his sister. No one there was to ever know. She was very hurt by this. She had looked forward to attending school with her brother and becoming more involved in his life again. He had begun to distance himself from her in his teen years. He seemed ashamed of her. He was no longer the brother he had been to her in their early childhood. Sidonie told her mother the next day what her brother had said. Her mother did not seem to think there was anything wrong with that. The smile on her mom's face and her slight chuckle indicated that she even found it to be a bit amusing. Her mother had never cared how Sidonie felt about anything. Her brother did not acknowledge her at school. He pretended as though he had no idea who she was. After the first few days of school, Sidonie realized that her brother had befriended the popular students. Apparently, he was concerned that she would ruin that for him as he struggled not to feel as though he was all the negative things their dad had been telling him his entire life. Her distant cousins and other students that she had known during her early childhood all acknowledged her. She noticed that her brother did not acknowledge many of them either.

Sidonie's first weeks of high school were intimidating. With the normal social pressures of high school in addition to her insecurities about herself, it was difficult to navigate this new environment of judgmental peers. She did not belong with her family at home, and she did not belong with her peers at school except for her few friends. It would have been much easier had her brother helped her through this challenge, but he excluded her from his social life in his own struggle. As the year proceeded, her friend group grew larger which helped. She always had someone she could relate to and someone to understand her in different situations, except her home life. Every time Sidonie began to attempt to share with any of her friends something of her miserable home life, they looked at her in confusion. They dismissed her as though it was not as bad as what she was attempting to explain. She did not realize that people who did not experience or witness such behaviors could not comprehend such things occurring with someone they knew, especially Sidonie who had not portrayed any issues or emotional instability. She always seemed to be well together. She quit attempting to share such things with them. She literally had no one to confide in regarding any of it. She had to keep it all to herself and deal with it all alone. She was struggling to keep her head above water. It was suffocating and she felt herself sinking deeper and deeper inside of herself. It was very lonely and getting darker with the burdens becoming heavier.

During most of her teen years, anytime she and her parents were in a social situation where there were unfamiliar boys her age who were near, her mom would always sternly and accusatorily question her about those boys. Sometimes her dad would whisper to her mom immediately prior to her mom's questioning, indicating that her father had her mom investigate the situation. She would ask Sidonie if she knew them, who they were, and why they were looking at her. If she had known them, she would have at least greeted them from a distance. Sidonie had no idea why the boys were looking at her because she believed that no guy could possibly be interested in her in such a manner as her mom would indicate. Also, if boys were within her path of vision to family members, her mom would question her in the same manner as to why she was looking at the boys, when she was actually looking at her cousins farther away. With non-relative boys who her parents knew, they did not want them speaking with their daughter in a one-on-one conversation, only group conversations.

Sidonie was not allowed to have a boyfriend or talk to boys on the phone. Her father was very adamant about that, and her mom was very strict with enforcing it. It was like her parents expected her to get pregnant young like her mom had. Regardless of her past molestation, Sidonie was innocent in that regard, as she had no interest in being intimate.

She secretly had a boyfriend for two months in the early part of ninth grade. They only saw each other at school and on the bus ride. They were never alone, and Sidonie was comfortable with that. She quickly became annoyed with him when he began to put his arms around her often. He always wanted to be affectionate with her. She was not comfortable with that. She felt like he probably wanted a more serious relationship. Sidonie definitely did not want that. She finally broke up with him because she could no longer tolerate him and did not want to hate him, which he made very difficult with his reaction to the breakup.

A few months later she was allowed to attend a Christmas party with others her age at the home of friends of her parents. Her ex-boyfriend was there and so was a girl who had been having a crush on him. He attempted to convince Sidonie to be his girlfriend again. His final attempt was to provide an ultimatum.

If she would not be his girlfriend, he was going to begin seeing the other girl. The other girl was standing next to him as he stated that to Sidonie. Sidonie did not care. She no longer liked him even as a friend. She could not tolerate him. The other girl smiled widely as Sidonie rejected him again. He then turned to the other girl to begin his relationship with her as Sidonie walked away. Sidonie had been friends with that girl for years. She could not understand how she was willing to accept being second choice for any guy. Sidonie had serious insecurities about herself, but she would not have accepted being anyone's second choice. If she had been in the other girl's position, she would have rejected him after that ultimatum. That girl had never seemed to have any insecurities and had a stable, calm home. Sidonie's family knew her family and all their neighbors whose homes were very close to each other. There was no drama at her home. Sidonie was very surprised at the other girl's lack of self-respect, but she was proud to have her own.

Her parents have always believed that their strictness prevented Sidonie from any intimacy with boys. However, Sidonie knew how easy it would have been to do so where she lived. She could have done many things against her parents' will without their knowledge. She had thought of many such things throughout her high school years. She had the ability to be deceitful and creative with believable stories to cover the truth. She could have done so convincingly as she had been taught and forced to by her parents to hide the misery in their home. She did not have that innocence, but Sidonie chose to not do such things. That was not the person she wanted to be.

Sidonie and her brother had walked far along the beach in front of their home many times. Above the beach were many trees close together. Being home alone as much as she was during her teens and knowing when and the length of time she would be home alone, Sidonie could have easily met a boy along the beach with plenty of places to hide within the trees. With their closest neighbor being a far distance away, a boy could have even gone into their home without her parents ever knowing. There were a couple of boys who would have been willing to make such efforts as they really wanted to be with her. She was not ready for that level of a relationship and knew she was not ready. She had a goal to be intimate with only one guy her entire life. She knew by observing other relationships that she would not find that such person in her early high school years. All those relationships had failed. Once she learned the concept of "sweet sixteen," Sidonie also had a goal of being sweet sixteen. However, her mom was not aware of any of this and would not have believed that of Sidonie. She judged Sidonie according to herself when she was a teenager. Her mother always made Sidonie feel like she had done something very wrong and bad, even when she was completely innocent of that of which she was being accused. With the way her mom treated her regarding boys, she made Sidonie feel as though she perceived her as a seductress eager to be intimate. Sidonie despised that. It made her feel as though she was a bad person and her mom hated her. In addition to her childhood sexual abuse, this also had some effect on Sidonie's intimate life when she later had one, and even a few years into her marriage.

As Sidonie entered high school, she began to barely see the light at the end of the very long, dark tunnel in which she was living. She knew she had the opportunity to eventually reach that light to her freedom from the abuse and extreme control, but it seemed very far away. She could not realistically imagine reaching it and did not know if she could make it to that light. From the age of 14 to 17, Sidonie was in a state of severe depression. She spent most of her time at home in her bedroom sobbing into her pillow. One somber evening, she sat motionlessly in the bathtub of warm, comforting water. Emotionally numb and desperate to escape her tormented life, she grasped the razor, which she used to shave, and examined it in effort to determine how she could use it to slit her wrist. Then, she considered failing in her attempt to end it all and the potential consequences of that failure. Her parents would have never considered any responsibility for their child's despair. Their children were not allowed to have any issues with anything their parents did. They believed children always had to be the problem, not the parents. In their roles as parents, they could never be at fault for any issues their children might have. It was always their children's responsibility to obey, accept, and be happy with whatever their parents inflicted upon and demanded of them. Those consequences enforced on her by her parents for such an attempt would have made her life even worse, and she would never have been allowed a moment alone for the possibility of another attempt. There were more moments such as these for Sidonie within the next few years considering other methods. The fear of the consequences of failing is the only reason she never attempted.

It was during this time that Sidonie began to write poetry. That was the only way she was capable of expressing her emotions. She could more accurately explain what she was experiencing with the use of metaphors, similes, personification, analogies, and imagery. That was her way of releasing some of what she had held inside probably her whole life. She wrote her poetry when she felt the need for emotional release, and it helped some each time. She used a specific notebook only for her poetry but did not tell anyone or allow anyone to read it.

While in ninth grade, Sidonie realized she sometimes spoke to people a little rudely, perhaps even a bit degrading. She recognized it as her dad's behavior in the way she often heard him speak to others. She did not want to treat people in such a manner. That was the first aspect Sidonie noticed about herself that she did not like and believed she could change. She focused on being more aware of how she spoke to people. Initially, she would notice immediately after speaking in that manner and quickly apologize. Then, she began to notice before speaking in that manner and would say it differently. In time, it became natural for her to speak better to people. She no longer had to be mindful of that. She continued to pay attention to her behaviors, changing the aspects of herself which she did not like, one at a time. She did this vigorously for years until she felt she had become the better person she wanted to be. Then, she continued to do so on occasion as she would discover something new she disliked while analyzing herself.

She had two friends throughout high school whose homes she was sometimes allowed to spend nights and even weekends. This was very beneficial to Sidonie. She was able to witness how families should be and that abuse in the home was not normal. She learned much from her time with these families as she became like a part of them. She was also able to take trips with them and have experiences beyond the limitations of the small-town area in which she had always lived. She learned more about the world and people.

Although a very good student, Sidonie had never liked school and never wanted to be there. She suddenly found herself not wanting to leave at the end of the school day. She then disliked being at home more than she disliked being at school. When she was sixteen, her mom asked her what was wrong. It took all those years of drowning in much despair for her mom to realize that her daughter was sad and to possibly care. Too much had accumulated for Sidonie to know where to begin, and she did not trust her mom to not make it worse for Sidonie, so she responded that nothing was wrong and confirmed that when asked again by her mom.

Sidonie's parents always held her brother somewhat responsible for her. As an adult, her brother attempted to parent her, but he followed the dominant example they had of doing so, which consisted of psychological abuse. Therefore, she would not confide anything in him, and he did not seem to know much of what was occurring in Sidonie's life. He did not seem interested in what she might be dealing with. That treatment continued into her adulthood and did not stop until she stopped it.

At the age of fifteen, Sidonie's mom left her husband again because of a matter regarding his behavior toward their son. Sidonie's brother moved out of the home and on his own as a result of that incident. Sidonie and her mom lived with family for two weeks. When her mom informed Sidonie that she had decided to return to her husband, Sidonie was very upset. She was just beginning to relax. She was no longer having to live in constant, heavy tension, and her mom was treating her much better. It was as though her resentment toward Sidonie was gone. She begged her mom not to return. Her mom did not want to continue living with family as she was an adult and felt the need to have her own home. Sidonie insisted on getting a job to help her mom pay bills for them to get their own place. Ultimately, her mom was afraid of not succeeding on her own and feared being solely responsible for Sidonie while in her care. She was concerned that if something were to happen to Sidonie while in her care, she would be blamed for it. Sidonie had no choice. She very reluctantly returned with her mom to the misery.

Some guy expressed their interest in Sidonie

during high school, but they were not her type. She could not share that same interest with them and could not have a boyfriend anyway. These guys were too different from Sidonie and the type of guys with whom she was familiar. They could not have related well with each other.

Still at the age of fifteen, a family friend from Sidonie's early childhood reentered their lives after his divorce. He was younger than her parents, but much older than Sidonie. A year later, there was an incident wherein he surprised Sidonie with an inappropriate kiss. She was very uncomfortable at that moment and knew it was wrong of him. Her immediate thought was to tell her parents in the next room. Then, as always, she considered the consequences. Her mom would have found some way to blame Sidonie and excuse his behavior with the fact that he was intoxicated with alcohol at that moment. Her mom would have insisted that she should not have allowed it to occur regardless of the fact that she had no warning. Her father would have trusted her mom's assessment of the situation to be accurate.

Her mom had always held Sidonie accountable for every wrong in which she was somehow involved and had always been partial to the males in their lives. Her mom raised her daughter to believe that females always had some fault in wrongs committed by males.

Sidonie's dad always seemed to trust his wife regarding their daughter in matters involving boys, perhaps because she had been a teenage girl herself, but she had not been this one. She really did not know her daughter and made no attempt to know her daughter, although she believed she knew Sidonie best. Her mom seemed to judge her based on how she, not her daughter, had been at that same age. After analyzing the potential consequences and not willing to suffer them, Sidonie chose to not say anything to anyone. She hoped that because of his drunken state, he would forget and never attempt such a thing again.

During that following year, that older guy, Damas, began doing things for Sidonie that most parents would have interpreted as suspicious and with wrong intentions. He brought her an expensive gift from one of his work trips. He also loaned her his automobile to commute to her local family member's homes while he and her parents were away for a couple of days. Then, he loaned it to her again one day for her commute to and from school. He progressed to phone conversations with her when calling to speak with her parents while she was the only one home. Her parents had brought a predator into her life. In her naiveness, Sidonie was clueless of this. Her parents seemed to be clueless as well.

Her mom had not lived a typical teenage nor early adult life to understand such things. Her father trusted a friend who he knew had and continued to take advantage of many adult aged girls and women, including one only two or three years older than Sidonie. He should have known that his daughter would not be considered an exclusion of that to such a person. Sidonie believed him to be a good guy since her parents were so fond of him. Eventually, Damas gained her interest beyond a family friend. Then, he suggested she call him when she was alone. They spoke on the phone for approximately a year. In some of those conversations, he would plan their future together, something she had not given any thought to. She had not been the type of girl who planned her future wedding or adult life. She was focused on reaching adult age to exit her childhood home and misery for college. He convinced her that they would one day marry, have children, and build a life together.

At the age of sixteen, Sidonie witnessed another argument between her parents, which was common. Her mom was in the kitchen and her dad in the living room. There was no dividing wall. It was open between the two rooms. Sidonie was in the kitchen with her mom when she heard her dad threaten to hit her mom, something he had not done in many years. The instant she heard that, all the fear Sidonie had ever had in her life disappeared. She stood between the two rooms, looked her dad directly in his eyes as she sternly told him that he would never hit her mom again because he would have to hit her first, then he would never see her again. He recognized that she meant every word of what she had said. She had witnessed her mom being beaten, jerked around, thrown against the wall, and drug on the ground by her hair. She would no longer allow it. For the first time ever, her dad took her seriously. He calmed down some as he said a few more much less harsh things. Sidonie responded with confirmation of her serious determination. Then, his attitude went back to normal. That is when all physical abuse from her dad against anyone in their home permanently ended.

One school day in tenth grade, Sidonie suddenly developed some difficulty breathing in class. She felt that she was not able to breathe deeply enough. It was as though she was not getting adequate oxygen. Otherwise, she felt fine. This concerned her as she had never experienced anything such as that. She informed the teacher then went to the office. She contacted her mom at her grandmother's home. Her mom was hesitant to do anything. She attempted to convince Sidonie that nothing was wrong with her. She was probably hoping that was true. However, she ended the call leaving Sidonie to believe that she was going to get her. Sidonie's mom, all of her family, and the school staff knew that Sidonie did not claim to be sick when she was not. She had never done that.

Time passed as Sidonie waited for her mom. She checked the time and realized her mother should have already arrived. It was a while longer before she was called to the office to check out. When she walked into the office, she did not see her mom. Her grandmother had come to get her and take her to visit the doctor. She learned that her mom did not have the money to pay for a doctor's visit or medication. She refused the money that her own mother offered, so Sidonie's grandmother chose to take Sidonie for a visit with the doctor against her own daughter's wishes. The doctor diagnosed Sidonie with bronchitis. Her grandmother had the prescription for Sidonie's medication filled then brought her home. Sidonie has always appreciated her grandmother for that. If she had not received treatment soon enough, Sidonie could have gotten much more ill resulting in hospitalization. Her mom was thirty-three years old at this time. She should have known the importance of seeking medical treatment in that situation. She should not have hesitated to accept financial help from her own mother for that treatment.

Eventually, Sidonie's suspicious extended family members learned of her and Dumas' non-physical relationship from others and told her parents. It did not go well for either of them. The words her parents spoke of Dumas completely contradicted their previous years of behavior toward him. Therefore, she believed the issue was not Damas but the fact that they did not want her to have any boyfriend as they had always made very clear. They were forced to end all communications and her parents exiled him from their lives. Sidonie's mom always held her daughter responsible for that relationship. She assumed her daughter had initiated it.

As time went by, that light at the end of the tunnel became closer and closer. Sidonie's social life at school expanded. She was beginning to feel as though she might belong more. She gradually overcame her depression. A few years after finishing high school, she realized that she had been much more popular in school than she had realized. Although she was never accepted by the popular groups, they all knew her and so did most of the students. Most of them had perceived her as popular and snobby. They had no idea of her insecurities causing her to be afraid of initiating interaction with other students who she was not already social with, but she always spoke with people who directly spoke to her first. Sidonie had attempted to speak with a few of the popular students at different times. They looked directly at her then turned away without a word as if she did not exist. That amplified her feelings of being insignificant and worthless. She feared that from everyone, so she made no other initial effort with any student. Fortunately, there were many who initiated with her. Perhaps they recognized the timidness in her. She really enjoyed socializing with people and was not the least timid once acquainted.

When Sidonie reached the home stretch of her last year of high school, also six months before turning eighteen, she began to realistically imagine reaching that light at the end of the tunnel and was very eager to do so. In addition to being very strict, her parents ensured that she was also very sheltered, not knowing what she had already been exposed to in her early childhood. There was still much she needed to know about people and what life could be like in the world among the many different types of people. Her parents made sure everyone actively involved in her life knew there were certain things not to be even mentioned in Sidonie's presence. She was not prepared for life out in the world as she entered adulthood. It was a crash course for her, and it was psychologically and emotionally brutal.

When Sidonie was seventeen and a half years of age with her own transportation and little freedom, she and Damas crossed paths again after not having spoken in many months. They began secretly seeing each other. Months later, she turned eighteen, but not much changed for her with her parents or within their home. A few months later, she graduated from high school, became employed full-time, and took an opportunity to move out of her parents' home and into her own.

Chapter 3

Approximately seven months after Sidonie began seeing Dumas, she learned that for a few months in the early period of what she believed to be an actual relationship, he had an actual relationship with someone else. She felt very betrayed, unimportant, insignificant, unloved, worthless, and stupid. She ended it, which was very difficult for her because she knew that meant she would not be intimate with only one guy. There would be a second.

Upon turning eighteen, Sidonie began going to a nightclub. It was her second time there when a boy close to her age had her cousin introduce them. Her cousin began the introduction, and the boy completed it adding a bit of her personal information not commonly known. He seemed very comfortable with her and looked at her as if he already knew her on a personal level. She knew that he was subtly informing her that he had been making the effort to know as much about her as he could, and he was very charming as he did so. That was an indication that he would be pursuing her. That was their second introduction.

A few months prior, that guy, Chrétien, had introduced himself to her in a very charming and flirty manner with his girlfriend of a couple of years standing next to him. That was a warning for Sidonie; a warning to not trust him because he was most likely an unfaithful guy. Remembering that introduction in this current moment, she knew she had to be cautious with him.

In that second introduction, something about him was very familiar to her as if she had known him her whole life, but she had not known him. They had only known what they had heard of each other from others for the previous few years. She knew at that moment that she could fall for him easily, quickly, and deeply. She did not want that. She was determined to avoid the heartache he was sure to cause her. She very soon learned that his relationship had ended sometime prior to their second introduction.

During those early months of her eighteenth year, Sidonie was followed from the nightclub on her route home on two different occasions. The first time, a guy had followed her through her out-of-the-way route to the highway leading to her home. She was able to briefly see the guy in his automobile and did not recognize him or the automobile. It was obvious that he was not familiar with the long, winding highway to her home. She was able to lose him and arrive at home without him learning where she lived. After that incident, a family friend in law enforcement gave Sidonie a can of mace to keep with her for her protection in the event that she was ever attacked.

The second time she was followed, two of her older cousins and their wives were with her. They had all planned to spend the night at one of the cousins' homes instead of taking the longer trip to their homes. As Sidonie was driving them all to their destination, an unfamiliar car came up behind them. The headlights flashed as the car continued to follow closely. It was as though the driver was signaling her to stop. She had only ever seen one car of that type and it was not that color. The driver had to see the additional four people in the car with her through her car window as their headlights shined brightly inside. The driver should have also been able to determine that two of the people in her car were men. Her two cousins were about to have Sidonie stop the car for them to confront the person as she approached a fork in the road. The car passed her then drove onto the road that was part of a route to her home. As she continued onto the other road, the car stopped, turned around, and traveled back in the direction from which it came. It was as though the person following her knew at least the area in which she lived and expected her to take that route. The windows of that car were dark. She could not see anything inside and wondered if there was one person or more in that car. She also wondered if she knew anyone in that car. She assumed she did not as she never saw that car again anywhere nor did anyone say anything about traveling behind her that night.

A month after ending her relationship with Damas, Sidonie began seeing another guy who had been pursuing her for a few months. He was a few years older than Damas. He was wonderful to her. He treated her as his equal, not younger. By then, she had become aware of the concept of daddy issues and analyzed herself for that possibility but could not see that it applied to her. She had been having older people tell her she was psychologically mature for her age since she was twelve. That was likely a result of all the expectations her mom had placed upon her to always be responsible and make no mistakes. Also, she was raised with an extended family of mostly older boys who were like brothers to her. She was like their baby sister. That may be why she was comfortable with and had an interest in older, mature guys. She could relate to them. The combination of both her maturity and social familiarity with older guys may have been the reason older guys had such interest in her.

That relationship was great, except for the fact that he was ready to settle down and create a family of his own. Sidonie was just beginning to really live. She had much more free living to do before she would be ready for that. This is what ultimately caused that relationship to end after a few months, but they remained dear friends who continued to trust and confid in each other.

At that time, Chrétien made his move, but only to be intimate with her. He did not succeed because they were not even seeing each other. She would not be intimate with a guy she was not in a relationship with. Chrétien knew that. Every guy did. He had not attempted to establish any meaningful relationship with her. She was interested in him, but not to be used.

As Sidonie began getting out into the world more and expanding her social life, she began to realize that many people seemed to already know her. She eventually became aware that her older cousins had been speaking of her to others at times throughout her teenage years. They were very proud of her and shared that. Some of their friends remembered her from her childhood when they would hang out with her cousins at their family homes, and they had also been speaking of her. Many people, especially guys, seemed anxious to meet her and get to know her more, then continued to want to be in her company. She felt almost like a princess making her debut but on a lesser scale. These people also protected her from the wrong things which others were doing and many of them were doing themselves. They did not expose her to drugs or any bad behaviors and did not allow others to expose her to such things. It was as though they did not want her to be tainted. They wanted to preserve her innocence that remained and her goodness. All this was very good for her very damaged self-esteem. However, it also created envy from many girls.

When Sidonie arrived somewhere or walked up to a group of people, all attention went to her. She did not know what was special about her to receive this reaction. She never perceived herself as being better or more special than others. The girls around in those moments strongly disliked the attention Sidonie received. They especially disliked the attention of their boyfriends being taken from them and given to Sidonie. She felt bad for them, but it was not her fault, and she did not know how to deal with those situations to eliminate that problem. She did learn how to manage such situations as she got a little older, but that did not help with the envy of all. She knew that had those girls known what her life had been like and continued to be like, they definitely would not have envied her. Their dislike of her did not help with her self-esteem. They seemed to attempt to find ways to ruin her reputation with false accusations of her being with guys and claiming she said things about others that she had not. Fortunately, all the guys, as well as the girls who liked Sidonie, knew those accusations were not true. It helped that the guys who she was accused of being with were honest about those accusations. The irony of the expansion of her social life is that her brother had not wanted anyone to know she was his sister for some time and now she was becoming friends with many people he had been friends with, and they seemed to enjoy her company more, some even told her they liked her more.

Sidonie began seeing another guy a month after the second relationship. He was close to her age and had also pursued her, but Sidonie was not sure that she could feel the same about him as he did her. A month in, he began to persist that she meet his mom and would not accept her polite refusal. She perceived meeting a parent to be somewhat serious. She still did not know if she could feel that way about him. She had not been intimate with him, even though he had made that effort, and felt that he was pressuring her for something more serious for which she was not ready. For some reason, that prompted Sidonie to stop seeing him and return to her relationship with Damas in which she was comfortable, especially since she already knew his parents. She was back with him for a couple of months.

By this time, Sidonie's self-worth and self-esteem had been severely damaged for years. She believed that she was a bad person, stupid, and had no common sense. During her childhood, she had gone from being outgoing to timid and sometimes withdrawn out of fear of others seeing the bad which her mom and brother saw in her or fear of doing or saying something stupid, resulting in others realizing that something was wrong with her mental function. She did not know how to verbally express herself on a deeper level as she had not been allowed to do so without harsh, degrading consequences. She felt completely worthless, unimportant, insignificant, and alone in the world. The contradiction of many extended family members and others often saying she was smart and a good child and teenager did not overcome the damage done to her by her immediate family, nor did all the love and positive attention from extended family members of all ages.

Abuse from a parent is the most devastating and impairing.

Soon after Sidonie graduated high school, someone new entered her life. Her new friend, Camille, must have sensed something familiar in Sidonie because she was eager to befriend her. Camille had noticed some of the negative behavior from Sidonie's mom and brother toward Sidonnie. Shortly after becoming friends, Camille shared a similar childhood experience of sexual abuse with Sidonie. In that moment, all the suppressed memories of Sidonie's childhood returned in a flood. She then mentally relived the trauma of her sexual abuse and was devastated by it. Now eighteen with fully developed comprehension, she considered that it may have been better for her had those memories remained suppressed, but she soon realized that those experiences were the reasons for many of her issues.

Sidonie had hated herself almost her entire life because of this abuse. She believed this was the sole reason for her severely damaged self-esteem and little self-worth, when she had any. She felt dirty, damaged, beneath almost everyone, and incapable of being loved. Upon remembering this abuse, she also blamed herself for allowing that abuse of her to occur. She believed she had done terribly wrong, was a horrible person, and did not deserve any good in life. Sidonie had always felt that she needed to work extra hard to just be averagely good and had no room for error. She believed she had to always get everything right to not be the worst person in the world.

Sidonie had begun her teens trusting her mom to know best for her and following her direction. By the time Sidonie reached the middle of her teen years, she realized that her mom's direction had not served her well in most situations. Her mom had been wrong about most matters, and Sidonie's initial thoughts of how she should deal with those matters would have had better results. It was then that Sidonie recognized that it would be beneficial for her to make her own decisions about her life as she would make better ones for herself. She now had the opportunity to move from her parents' home. She confidently took her freedom and independence which her parents were still refusing to give her. She had finally reached the bright light and was out of the dark tunnel. From that moment, she was determined to make her own decisions based on what she needed, what was best for her, and what worked for her life. That is when Sidonie began to fight for control over her own life and to simply be her, not who anyone wanted her to be.

It was very soon after the return of those childhood memories of abuse that Sidonie moved out of her childhood home. She had finally reached the end of that tunnel but soon realized that she was still living in darkness, now of a vast space. Removing herself from the environment of abuse and house of memories of that abuse freed her from it all, but not the damage from any of it. Without the burden of negative emotions from that home, she immediately began actually dealing with her trauma. Removing herself seemed to instinctively prompt her to do so. She somehow knew that she needed to deal with and overcome her issues to be able to become fully functional and have a good future in which she could be happy. Her main goal in life since her early teen years was to have a good, happy future unlike her childhood, as she could not live her entire life unhappy and miserable as she always had.

She began the process by repeatedly reliving her trauma over time. That was brutally painful, but she desperately needed to understand why she allowed it to occur all those times. After reliving it a few times, Sidonie realized that she was remembering the events in her current perception with fully developed comprehension. She needed to remember the perception of that young child. She went deep and remembered what she was like as that young child; what she was thinking and feeling in each moment of each incident and how her brain processed every contributing factor. Once she remembered the thought process of that very young child, she was finally able to forgive herself. This process was not a short one and did not immediately resolve all her issues resulting from this abuse, but it was progress. Upon the return of those memories of her sexual abuse, she believed that was the reason for all her issues. It was not until later that she began to realize the massive dark cloud under which she had been struggling through life.

Dumas was not happy about Sidonie moving from her parents' home. She initially did not understand why because they now had more freedom to see each other. Sidonie soon realized that he did not want her to have her freedom. He wanted her to remain under her parents' strict control so that she had little opportunity to discover all the wrong he had been doing to her. She became aware that her suspicion of not being the only girl he was with, besides his other relationship, was correct. She learned that she had always been one of many. He had preyed on her, then used her the entire time. He had even brought her into his parents' lives in the beginning. He had been thorough. She finally accepted the truth of what she had believed to be a relationship and ended it without any resistance from him. The reality of his complete disregard for her amplified her already existing issues.

Sidonie was very hurt that Dumas would treat her with such disregard. She was drinking at a nightclub one night. One of her cousins was there with his long-term girlfriend. She and Sidonie had become close. She did not like Sidonie being treated as such and hurt like that. Her way of dealing with such situations was different from Sidonie's. Her way was more about revenge. Sidonie had drank a bit much alcohol and was tipsy. Dumas' automobile was parked in front of the building near the door. The girl was older than Sidonie. She asked Sidonie where her keys were, then told her to take them out. Sidonie did as told. The girl explained to Sidonie how to place her car key between two of her fingers holding the remaining keys in the grip of her hand. Sidonie did not know why she was instructing her to do that. The girl then guided Sidonie to Dumas' automobile. She placed her hand around Sidonie's hand, lifted Sidonie's hand holding the key, and guided Sidonie along the side of the automobile as the girl applied pressure to the key. As the girl lifted the key to the automobile, Sidonie realized what the girl was going to do. Sidonie had heard of people keying automobiles, but she would have never done anything like that herself. She would not damage anyone's property. She should have stopped it then, but she was young, the girl was her elder even if not by very many years, and she was not thinking as clearly as she did without the effects of alcohol. Sidonie disagreed with the manner in which the girl was attempting to help Sidonie feel better, but she appreciated the fact that the girl cared for her that much to want her to feel better.

The next day, Dumas' mother informed Sidonie that Dumas was very upset when he noticed the damage to his automobile, not knowing Sidonie was involved. He did not notice that night when he left the nightclub. Sidonie did not tell anyone about the girl's involvement when she confided in her closest friends about the incident as she did not want the girl to get into any legal trouble because of her caring intention toward Sidonie. Sidonie accepted full responsibility because she knew Dumas would not do anything legally or otherwise regarding Sidonie because of his relationships with her family. He did not want any of them to know what he had done to her. She considered he might find out she was involved as she could not be sure that no one had seen them do it. She felt bad about the damage to Dumas' automobile, but not guilty as she did not apply any pressure to the key. The girl completely controlled it, and Sidonie would have never done such a thing. Although she took responsibility for it, she did not actually feel responsible. She felt that the girl would have probably done it herself alone anyway had Sidonie refused to participate.

Sidonie's social life was continuing to expand. Most people thought very positively of her and that she was a good person. She was not the type to be influenced. She perceived persistence of influence as a lack of respect for her right to make her own choices. She had been dismissed by her family enough throughout her childhood. She was not going to allow it from others in this regard. Anytime anyone persisted in influencing her, she got angry and wanted to leave the situation. That is when it became known to accept her choice. Sidonie also became aware that she had acquired a reputation as a good girl in her small hometown area where everyone knew everyone and all their business. She could not have hidden anything she did if she had attempted. Having this favor also helped her progress since those people had to know enough about her to know what type of person she was. She eventually became more popular among and accepted by all classes of society with a much better reputation than her brother. That was not a goal of hers. It simply occurred. Her brother had attempted to make her appear stupid to others and inferior, but the genuine truth of who she was showed through. Her brother's shame of her became envy and more resentment.

Sidonie did very well living on her own that young. She had the freedom to do whatever she wanted whenever she wanted. No one had authority over her. She chose to remain responsible. She did not really do anything on weekdays. She was always in bed at a good time to be rested for work the next day. She maintained her morales and lived by them. She was told by an older friend that some of them had expected Sidonie to go wild. Those people had known how strict and sheltered Sidonie's life had been. They were surprised that Sidonie did not go wild as most in such situations had done. However, Sidonie was too responsible.

Any minor mistake Sidonie made resulted in her getting very upset with and hating herself. She would feel this way when her keys were not where she always kept them, which was very seldom. Her expectations of herself were too high. Camille always misplaced her keys and spent time looking for them. She always laughed about it as if it was not a concerning matter. Sidonie could not understand her being so irresponsible. Sidonie was getting extreme about such matters. Had it not been for Camille's unintentional influence, Sidonie would have probably had a nervous breakdown at some point. Eventually, Sidonie realized that she did not need to take such matters so seriously. She learned to relax some. As Camille stated to Sidonie many years later, they balanced each other. Sidonie learned to not take minor matters so seriously and Camille became more responsible.

Camille also benefited Sidonie in other ways.

There were a couple of moments when Camille informed Sidonie of the reason Sidonie had negatively reacted to a situation as she did, and Camille was exactly correct. She was the first person to ever truly know Sidonie. Because of that, Sidonie began to believe Camille when she contradicted the behaviors of Sidonie's mom and brother toward Sidonie and explained that Sidonie was not the problem. They were wrong about her. Sidonie was not a bad or stupid person.

Chrétien began pursuing Sidonie. He seemed to love the feistiness she had acquired out of need from being smaller than most, in addition to being raised with older cousins who loved to tease her for a reaction. Being that petite resulted in some of her peers attempting to intimidate her as they thought it would be easy. She had to be feisty and prepared to defend herself to prevent such behavior. Chrétien was amused by that feistiness as many guys were, and he would sometimes affectionately provoke her. It was an interesting and exciting dynamic. He was the only one to ever really know how to truly deal with her in the correct way to receive her cooperation in her feisty moments.

Every time his ex-girlfriend was at the same location as he and Sidonie, she would stand near them observing their every interaction. She would not stand close enough to hear what was said between them, but close enough to make her glaring presence known. Chrétien would tell Sidonie he really cared about her and beg her to give him a chance. As soon as she would agree, he would insist he had to leave and would do so with his friends. After a couple of those times, he actually stayed to spend time with her. He had her take him to another location as he wanted to see who was there. He decided to go inside for a drink and insisted she wait for him in the car because he would not be long.

After a couple of minutes, Sidonie decided she did not want to wait in the car, so she went inside. There were not very many people there. Upon entering, she saw him standing at the bar with his ex-girlfriend standing next to him. They were talking. Those two and the ex-girlfriend's sister were the only three people at the entire bar. She thought that of all the space around the bar, he had to go stand next to her. Perhaps she had gone to stand next to him. Sidonie would never know. She immediately realized that he had probably recognized an automobile that one of them drove in the parking lot and knew his ex-girlfriend was there. Sidonie felt there was still something significant between the two, and she never wanted to interfere with any relationship or potential for one. She briefly stood completely still and in shock as she processed the situation. Then, she turned around, walked out, and left. He never saw her inside the building. She did not leave him stranded as she knew he had a ride with his ex-girlfriend.

A few weeks later, the boyfriend of Camille arrived at their home with Chrétien. Those two guys had been childhood friends and were close friends. Camille's boyfriend had made plans with Camille to spend the night, which meant Chrétien would also be spending the night. He made an advance toward Sidonie again. By then, she really wanted to be with him in a meaningful relationship, but he still had not made any effort to establish anything near that. She knew that he had the power to break her heart worse than anyone had or could at that time, as she had developed feelings for him of a depth she had never before experienced. It was very difficult for her to resist him, but she ultimately did. She was terrified that casual intimacy was all he wanted from her. If that were so, she would have been crushed had she shared herself with him in such a way. As the guys were preparing to leave the next morning, Sidonie gave Chrétien her phone number. He kissed her goodbye and left. She perceived that kiss goodbye as promising. She thought they might finally begin seeing each other.

Two weeks later, Sidonie had still not heard from him. She inquired about that with Camille's boyfriend and learned that Chrétien was not allowed to make long distance phone calls since he had made many in the past resulting in a large bill. She decided to call him in an attempt to subtly discern his true intention with her. His older brother, Jacques, answered and informed her that Chrétien was not there. As she attempted to end the call, he continued the conversation. Each time she attempted to end the call after that, he again continued the conversation. They had met once before. It was not pleasant as she determined him to be too assertive of which she impolitely made him aware. She had no idea Jacques and Chrétien were brothers. She also had no idea that Jacques was the person she was speaking with on the telephone as she did not remember his name. Later, she realized that he must have remembered her name and knew that it was Sidonie he was speaking with because he insisted on visiting that afternoon as he had to travel to the area for another reason. She trusted it would be okay because he was Chrétien's brother and friends with her cousin. She agreed but did not expect him to go. He did.

Upon his arrival, she immediately recognized him. It was a pleasant visit. It seemed that he was being a friend to her. Without sharing any details, she subtly inquired about Chrétien's intentions as she thought his brother would be the person most likely to know of their situation. His response was that was how Chrétien was. She understood what he meant by that. He was indicating that Chrétien had a history of using girls for casual intimacy. That told her what she needed to know, although she secretly maintained a bit of hope that the situation with her was different, and he had genuine feelings for her. Jacques seemed to be a friend helping pick up the pieces his younger brother had left. Another week passed and she still had not heard from Chrétien. During that week, Jacques called Sidonie and visited again, securing their friendship.

Chrétien knew that she was often at the same nightclub on weekends. It was not difficult for him to see her locally to him if he chose. That is where she was that Friday night with her best friend. Hoping for the last time that he would make an effort and arrive at that location, Sidonie hung out with Jacques as her new friend. Chrétien never presented. She left the nightclub that night having given up on anything meaningful developing between she and Chrétien and determined to move on, but she had no intention of moving on with anyone at the time.

Jacques was not in the best condition to drive. That is what he convinced Sidonie. She offered to drive him, and he agreed. As they were leaving, he did not let her drive, but insisted she help him by shifting the gears. She thought she would be driving him to his home with Camille following as she was Sidonie's ride home. However, he did not want to go to his home with his parents and insisted on spending the night at Sidonie's and Camille's home. After arriving at their home, Sidonie made a place for him to sleep on the living room floor then turned to go to her bedroom. Much to her surprise, Jacques made an advance toward her. She thought of him only as a friend. She initially attempted to pull away, but he was persistent.

She did not know why she decided to be with him that night. Sidonie had never been intimate with a guy she was not already in a relationship with. Perhaps it was the rejection by Chrétien, which had caused her already existing issues to amplify just as they had begun to fade. She was feeling completely alone in the world again, as well as, unwanted, incapable of being loved, damaged, and worthless. She also had, in the past, believed that no decent guy would ever want to be with her. She was feeling that way again, and this guy wanted to be with her. He seemed to want something real with her. Regardless of the reason, she was sure there would never be any real chance of anything meaningful with Chrétien. Otherwise, she definitely would not have been with his brother.

The next night, Sidonie and Camille went to the nightclub again, where Camille's boyfriend was to meet them. He again arrived with the Chrétien who went straight to Sidonie. He told her he was going home with her that night. He was a night too late as she had already given up on him and moved on with someone else, his brother. She responded by sternly asking him why. She was wondering why, after three weeks of absolutely no contact and no effort, he showed up to spend the night with her. It had to be a second attempt at a casual intimate encounter. He responded by sternly confronting her about being with his brother the night before. It all became clear to Sidonie then. Camille had told her boyfriend about Sidonie and Jacques, and he told Chrétien. That is why he went that night. He must not have believed that she had actually gone through with being with his brother in that manner and was concerned that Jacques might succeed with her before he did. Sidonie perceived it as more of a competition for him. She knew any further conversation with him at that moment would be pointless. He would only see her wrong and not what he had done to her. He had broken her heart. She had been so good at hiding her emotions that she was able to hide that from everyone. She did not want him to know because he would have then known how easy it would have been for him to get the casual encounter he most likely wanted. He would have known exactly what to say and exactly what to do to convince her that he had genuine feelings for her, all just to get what he wanted. This is what she had learned from her experience with Damas. She attempted to learn all that she could from each experience in her life. Now, she was attempting to protect herself. This is also why she had been cautious not to let him know that her feelings for him were deep. However, in all her efforts to protect herself, she failed. She had been hurt as badly as she would have been had she been intimate with him. Knowing that the conversation would accomplish nothing, she walked away from him and onto the dance floor. Sidonie had always loved to dance. When she was on the dance floor, everything completely faded away, including all her problems and negative emotions. She did not see Chrétien again that night. He must have left shortly after the confrontation.

Sidonie's encounter with Jacques was the beginning of a brief relationship. That was a relief to her because it was not a one-time intimate encounter, which was against her strong morales. She did not have that on her conscience. She had known nothing about Jacques prior to their first visit at her home. Then, she only knew what he had told her. She quickly began to learn more about him from others. He had, in the past, pursued his brother's, Chrétien's, girlfriend. He often pursued girls for casual intimate encounters.

Sidonie realized that his intention from the beginning was to be with her. He was not attempting to be only her friend. She was still naïve and had been played again. She felt really bad for Chrétien. Had she known this, she would have never spent time with Jaques. There would never have been anything between them, but it was too late then. The damage had been done. By then, she and Jaques were already connecting deeply. He trusted her enough to confide in her some of his deepest emotions and regrets. They developed a deep, strong friendship.

The relationship ended with him being unfaithful to Sidonie. He called her the very next day, not knowing that she already knew. He was honest about it and told her it was him, not her and he was messed up. She knew he had been struggling with life from the tears he had shed while confiding in her. He was as lost as she was, but self-destructive at times, which resulted in a guilty conscience. Sidonie had known him to always be honest with her, and she greatly appreciated that as she had been used to many lies and much deception with Damas. She was okay when she realized from their conversation that she would not be losing Jacque's friendship. She had not been in love with him. It was not the relationship she was struggling with losing, it was the friendship. He had been there for Sidonie in a way that no one else was and she really needed. He seemed to only see good in her. That was gradually changing the way she perceived herself.

He continued to be there for her in such a way, and her for him. They remained very close. That resulted in a few more intimate moments, but only when neither of them was in a relationship. She still struggled with this relationship ending because with the end of each relationship came the realization that she would be intimate with another. That number would increase one more and that really bothered her.

Sidonie knew that Chrétien could never be able to overcome her being with his brother, and she could not either. She had very strong morales and could not be someone who was ever with two people of relation at any point in time. During the time of her brief relationship with his brother, Chrétien began to look at Sidonie as if he hated her every time they saw each other anywhere. After her relationship with Jacques ended, Chrétien continued to look at her the same. That glare felt like a knife piercing her heart. At some point, she realized that she could overcome having been with his brother to be with him. He was the exception. For the first time in her life, she was willing to sacrifice one of her strongest morales, and it was to be with him. That was how deep her feelings for him were. She had been correct in her assessment of their second introduction. She had fallen for him very deeply and without much effort from him.

Sidonie was in one fight throughout her life. Not knowing how to express herself nor feeling the need to, she was sure people thought that fight was for a reason that it is was not. The ex-girlfriend of Camille's boyfriend had been trying to get back with him for months. That relationship had been over for some time before he and Camille began seeing each other. That girl was interfering with both Camille's and her boyfriend's lives in her effort. Camille was never going to confront her or attempt in any way to stop her. She was not the type, and that girl refused to accept his repeated rejection. That girl was also the girl with whom Jacques had been unfaithful to Sidonie.

One night, Sidonie was at a nightclub and so was that girl. A group of Sidonie's friends were there also as well as Jacques. These were older girls with whom Sidonie had family ties since she was very young. After Sidonie walked away to go to the bar, that girl went socialize with the same group of girls. She continually looked at Sidonie with a conniving smile as though she was taunting Sidonie. That girl then went to Jacques and spoke to him while continually looking at Sidonie with her conniving smile. Jacques also looked toward Sidonie as if uncomfortable in that situation. He ended the conversation quickly and walked away.

Sidonie was already aware of that girl having recently been hanging out with her cousin and other guy friends of Sidonie. She had also had an intimate encounter with Sidonie's first ex-boyfriend. This all occurred after Jacques had cheated with her. It seemed obvious to Sidonie that after taunting Camille for months, that girl was now taunting her. Some of these people were either family or like family to Sidonie and treated her much better than her immediate family. She needed them.

As the nightclub closed and everyone was leaving, Sidonie walked out with her group of friends. As they were walking through the parking lot to their automobiles, one of her friends informed Sidonie that conniving girl was attempting to get that friend to go to her car to speak with her, but her friend did not want to. She obviously was not interested in engaging with that conniving girl. Sidonie perceived that as an opportunity. She offered to go with her friend. They walked up to the passenger side window that was open. Camille's hair was naturally red. That conniving girl's hair was naturally blond, but she had occasionally had it dyed red in the past. She had recently dyed it red again. That conniving girl began speaking with Sidonie's friend. The moment Sidonie heard a pause in their conversation and pretending to be surprised, she stated to that girl that her hair was red. Then, in a patronizing manner, Sidonie asked that girl if she was trying to be like Camille. That girl immediately responded by leaning across the car and grabbing Sidonie's hair. That is when Sidonie began punching her.

That girl apparently had her car in drive with her foot on the brake because the car began to slowly move forward. Eventually, one of Sidonie's friends was able to open the driver door, stop the car, and set it to park. Then, another friend pried that girl's hand open to release Sidonie's hair for a third friend to pull Sidonie away from that girl. The third friend was twice Sidonie's size and strong. She had to pull Sidonie so hard that she fell on the ground and Sidonie fell on her. Sidonie stood up with praises from her assisting friends. That proved to Sidonie that their loyalty was to her, and she would not lose them to such a person as that girl. Sidonie then began to cry, which her friends could not understand as she had succeeded in that fight. What they did not understand is that even though Sidonie provoked the fight, she had not wanted to be provoked herself to go to that extent to stop someone from attempting to hurt her and Camille. She could not understand why that girl wanted to hurt either of them. They had not done anything to her. Sidonie blamed Jacques for his unfaithfulness more than that girl because he was the one in the relationship with Sidonie at the time. She did not provoke a fight with that girl over Jacques as people probably believed. She had reached her limit with people trying to hurt her and now take people from her.

Even as an independent adult, Sidonie's mom and brother regularly made her feel that she was a bad person who could never do good or right. They would always find something wrong with her or something she did, despite her constant efforts to be and do good. She had spent years analyzing herself so that she could correct whatever was wrong with her and be normal. She was still doing this and still could not see what they saw in her. Her mom sometimes told her that, as her mom, she knew her better than anyone, including herself. Sidonie believed that and assumed she was simply unable to see in herself what her mom saw in her, regardless of her determined efforts. She had spent almost the entire first eighteen years of her life looking for the bad in herself, never the good.

That year was ending. It was December when Sidonie saw her third cousin who she had grown up closely with as family. There was another guy there whom they had both known growing up. He was her brief, annoying boyfriend in ninth grade. Sidonie made plans with them both to all hang out the next weekend. She would not have hung out with the other guy alone because she knew he would have persistently attempted to be with her as he had demonstrated his continuing interest in her a few times over the years. With her cousin there, she knew she would be fine. He would prevent the guy from pursuing her.

The day for which these plans were made, Jacques, who she was still good friends with, called her stating that he and some friends would be hanging out in that area that night and might need a place to sleep. She offered her home. Her cousin arrived at her home that evening as planned. He entered alone with a bottle of liquor which she had never heard of. When she inquired where the other guy was, her cousin informed her that he had canceled on them for something else that arose. She found that odd as the guy was very eager for their plans, but she accepted that answer. Her cousin walked directly to the kitchen, removed a glass from the cabinet, and poured the liquor insisting she drink some. Not knowing anything about that liquor, Sidonie informed her cousin that she had a low tolerance for alcohol. He assured her that it had a low alcohol content. He only poured a small amount, but it was straight liquor. Trusting her cousin, Sidonie drank the liquor.

Something seemed a little strange with him from the moment he arrived, but Sidonie could not determine what it was. They left for their evening out. She was normally a very interactive, social person and somewhat affectionate, especially with family. She was a hugger, but that evening, she chose to be less friendly and not affectionate with him as she was a bit uncomfortable without knowing why. They hung out at a nightclub briefly before she began feeling ill. They returned to her home at which time she realized she was intoxicated. The drink he had given her was obviously not low in alcohol content. Upon entering her home, Sidonie went directly to the bathroom as she had become very ill. He followed her. As she was leaning over the toilet ill, he began to voice feelings for her, feelings inappropriate for family. Something about the way he was saying these things and his demeaner frightened her. She began to cry. Then, she remembered that Jacques might be coming to her home that night and stated, in her emotional voice with tears, that she wanted Jacques. She was desperately hoping Jacques would arrive at that moment.

Upon hearing Jacques' name, her cousin became angry. In his anger he asked, "Why him and not me?" She felt a hint of aggression in his anger. Sidonie cried more. She simply did not want to be in this situation and was hoping Jacques would arrive to end it. Once she felt she could, she stood up and walked to her bed to lie down as she was very weak. Her cousin followed her. He laid on top of her pinning her down as she stated “no” repeatedly. She placed her hands on his chest and attempted to push him off but to no avail. She did not have the strength to fight, and he was very strong and heavy. She continued to cry and say “no” and “don’t”. Then, she felt his hand moving up her thigh. In that instance, she knew another minute longer would probably be too late. The damage would be done, and she would not have been able to live with that, not with everything she had already been through and the issues which she was already dealing with. She quickly analyzed the situation. She realized that the more she cried and pleaded for him to stop, the more aggressive he became. She decided to attempt a calmer approach. She attempted to stop crying and speak in a normal, less emotional voice, as she asked, “Please don’t do this.” She looked into his eyes as she spoke. They were black and cold. A very strange thing occurred next. The very moment she finished her plea, his eyes went back to normal and opened very widely as if in shock as he immediately removed himself and stood up. It was as though he had been in a trance broken by her last words in their calm tone leaving him in shock over his own actions. He told Sidonie that he was leaving as he began to walk out of the room and toward the door to exit. He also said he would talk to her later and assured her he was locking the door behind him.

The very instant that door closed, Sidonie stepped out of her bed with haste and ran to the door, bolting then chaining it. She then looked at the doorknob to see if he had indeed locked it with concern that he intended to later return. Surprisingly, he had locked it. She returned to her bed and cried as hard as she ever had and could. She was devastated! Someone she had trusted her whole life to protect her presented to be the one who she needed protection from. She cried until she cried herself to sleep.

A couple of hours later, she was awoken by the ring of her phone. Barely awake and still devastated, Sidonie answered emotionally. She heard Jacques's voice, then began to cry again. He asked her if she had been drinking and apparently assumed that was why she was crying. That was strange since she had never cried when having consumed alcohol. On the contrary, alcohol somewhat numbed her negative emotions inhibiting her from crying. He informed her that they would be arriving soon and ended the call. She cried herself back to sleep to be awoken by a knock on her bedroom window and Jacques's voice. She had been sleeping too hard to hear the knock on the door as she always had. Upon waking, she began to cry again. She let them in and immediately walked back to her bedroom crying. Of the friends he had with him, she knew one well. He and Jacques both followed her to her room with concern. She sat on her bed crying so hard that she could not speak. Jacques left the room to join his other friends. That one friend remained, sitting at the foot of the bed on the corner to give her space and waiting patiently. When Sidonie was able to stop crying enough to be able to speak, she began to tell the friend what had occurred. She did not get very far into the events that had unfolded when he stood up and walked out of the room to Jacques. The friend had heard enough to have a good idea of what had occurred to Sidonie and relayed that to Jacques. Jacques then entered the room. She told him the whole story. Now he knew it was not the alcohol that had caused her to cry. He gave her some water, then prepared her something to eat and brought it to her. He was attentive, comforting, and took care of her. She will never forget the friend who knew there was something significant to the situation and sat patiently with her. It was at that moment that she knew the genuinely good, caring person he was. She will always appreciate him as a good friend.

The next day, she cried some more. She analyzed everything about that evening, including what she was wearing. She was desperately attempting to find a reason that he would have done that to her. She wanted to know if she had done something to contribute to his inappropriate feelings and actions.

That was the belief of girls being responsible for guys' inappropriate behaviors that her mom had instilled in her. She was wearing the same outfit she had worn to work at the office that day. It was not revealing or form-fitting.

Because of the uneasiness she felt with him from the moment of his arrival, she had remained somewhat disconnected toward him and less friendly with him compared to how she normally was. Sidonie should have canceled the plans then. She knew something was wrong but did not trust her intuition. Her mom had taught her that her intuition was always wrong, so she was to always dismiss it and think logically against it. Her mom believed her own intuition to be accurate, but Sidonie could never be correct about anything. She could not have intuition. Every concern Sidonie had was declared "in her head" by her mom, as though she would simply imagine it. She could not find anything that she had done to have led to her cousin's actions.

Camille was out of town with her boyfriend that weekend. Sidonie was terrified to stay home by herself that night in fear that her cousin would return. She spent that night at her aunt's home. The following day, Camille returned with her boyfriend. Sidonie cried again as she told them of the event. Camille's boyfriend informed her that the liquor was very potent.

It had a very high alcohol content. He was convinced that her cousin had planned the situation. She cried for a few more days about the incident and for many years every time she spoke of it, which was very seldom.

Two weeks later, she saw the other guy who was supposed to join her cousin and her that night. She inquired as to why he had canceled. He informed her that her cousin had told him those plans had altogether been cancelled. That was confirmation for her that her cousin had planned the event. He made sure to be alone with her. It is likely that he planned to get her intoxicated and take advantage of her. He may not have planned to rape her, but lost control of himself. Regardless, she now knew what he was capable of. She never again spent a night alone in that home. Everywhere she went, she analyzed her surroundings to make sure her cousin was not around. Sidonie eventually learned to trust her intuition. Sadly, it took the consequences of several bad situations for her to learn to do so.

A few months later, she learned that Chrétien had actually been very hurt by her relationship with his brother. His piercing glare was his pain. She had not seen him recently at this point in time. The next time she saw him, she saw red around the edges of his eyes as he spoke to her for the first time since that night he had confronted her. She was familiar with that indication of emotional pain. They did not speak about their situation. A couple of months later, he unexpectedly visited their home. Sidonie and Camille had moved to the area in which Chrétien and Camille's boyfriend both lived. That was also Sidonie's hometown area. Camille's boyfriend also moved in with them. She now had two roommates, and Chrétien had his friend as an excuse to visit. Upon entering their home, he immediately hugged her. After he sat in the chair at the kitchen table, he pulled her to him to sit on his lap. He remained affectionate with her throughout his visit and even asked her for a simple kiss, which she gave. She felt home in his arms. That was the first time she had felt that way with anyone. She knew then that she would go anywhere with him. His visit was not long. When he went to leave, she begged him not to go. As with all the other times, he insisted he had to go and did. Sidonie was sad because he still was not going to make her a priority. He was still not making the effort to establish anything more with her.

One night, Sidonie had gone to the nightclub with her two roommates. After returning home, they prepared for bed and settled in. Sidonie was in the process of falling asleep when she heard a noise at her bedroom window directly above the head of her bed where her head rested. She was afraid. Sidonie softly and quietly climbed out of bed and walked lightly to the doorway of the bedroom of her roommates. She whispered Camille's boyfriend's name and told him that she was hearing a noise at her window. He quietly climbed out of bed and carefully walked to the doorway of her bedroom. He also heard the noise. That window was next to the door through which they most used to enter and exit the house. He walked to that door being careful not to make any noise that would have alerted whoever was at the window. He quickly unlocked the door and opened it while turning on the outside light to hopefully catch the person before he could escape. That attempt failed. He saw no one. It took too long and was noisy to unlock and unchain the door prior to opening it. The person had a warning and time to run out of sight. It was very dark behind the house with pasture then field as far as could be seen in daylight.

The next day, Camille's boyfriend showed the girls his observation of the bent metal around the bottom of the screen on the window. That was clear evidence that someone had attempted to remove it to get to the window. He also noted that it had not been like that prior to that night because he would have noticed with the very close proximity to the door. They would have noticed if they had been followed home that night on the desolate highway then road leading to their home. Sidonie wondered if the person already knew where she lived and arrived after them, parked in the field and came through the pasture, or possibly arrived before them and waited in the dark behind the house. The person had to know there was a guy in the house. He would have seen him with her and her other roommate that night whether at the nightclub or entering the home. She considered the possibility of it being someone she knew not wanting to wake her roommates and with no intent to cause harm, but such a person would have softly knocked on the window and said her name. Sidonie now feared staying in that home alone at night. There was a possibility that the person could have been her cousin. He might have learned where she now lived and returned for a second attempt. Regardless of who the person was, she felt in danger.

A few weeks passed. By then, she had been taking drives down mostly deserted highways some evenings to break down emotionally. She would wait until it was dark so the occasional vehicle crossing her could not see her inside her car as she cried as hard as anyone possibly could. She would turn her radio very loud to drown out the loudest screams that she could bellow so no one would hear. She screamed and cried in agony. She begged God to take it all away and help her get beyond that suffering to where she needed to be. She knew timing was important for everything and trusted that God would get her where she needed to be in life in the right time, but she desperately needed him to help her get through the present. She also knew that if she were to have such a breakdown where anyone could see or hear her, she would be admitted for psychiatric evaluation and treatment. Sidonie simply could not confide all these things in anyone. She did not even know how to express it in words. She also could not miss work because she would not be able to pay her bills, and returning to live with her parents was not an option she could survive. This is when she quit writing poetry. She had already written all that she could express throughout the years. What was left was beyond words, so she put the notebook away. She was drowning in pain and loneliness. She could not bear both at the same time anymore. That is when she settled to at least eliminate the loneliness.

Sidonie began to see a guy who had been interested in her for a few months. In the very beginning, she was not sure how she felt about him. Sometimes, she really liked him. Other times, she did not like him at all. There were certain things she liked about him and certain things she did not. He wanted to move quicker in the relationship than what she was ready for. He invited himself to sleep over a couple of times during which she was not intimate with him because she was not ready. After only a couple of months and shortly after she was first intimate with him, he arrived as planned, but with some of his clothes. The guy, Benoni, went directly to her bedroom to place them as if he lived there. This had never been discussed and she did not want him leaving his things at her home. That was a clear indication to her that he was planning to spend many nights there. She did not want that but did not know how to tell him. Sidonie remembered hearing many times from older women that guys were afraid of commitment. In her attempt to resolve that situation by having him take his clothes back home with him, she told him he might as well move in. That was a huge mistake. She expected him to retract his action out of fear of commitment, but instead, he asked if she was sure. Sidonie did not know how to get out of that situation. She hesitantly maintained her disingenuous suggestion. She was afraid of confrontation in situations in which she could be responsible for hurting someone she felt did not deserve it, so she avoided such confrontations by going along. Although too much way too soon for Sidonie, Benoni moved in.

She was not happy with the situation. They did not get along well. A month later, she told him that living together was not working and he needed to move out. He did not deal well with that. He became angry in his disagreement. Still in constant emotional pain Sidonie was not ready to end the relationship because she could not deal with the loneliness in addition. She decided to spend the weekend at a friend's home, hoping Benoni would take her seriously and move out while she was gone. On the second night, she decided she wanted to sleep in her own home and returned after dark. He was not there but all his things were. He returned early the next morning after going out with a friend. Her efforts failed.

Chrétien presented in her life a few times within the following months. This did not go well with Benoni. He did not want Chrétien around Sidonie and aggressively informed him of that. Then, Chrétien began dating his ex-girlfriend. She also did not want the two around each other.

Sidonie's relationship with Benoni was doomed from the beginning. They lived together for approximately seven months. During that time, he got a job making enough money for her to quit her job to attend college as she had always planned. Then, he cheated on her with his ex-girlfriend. Sidonie was devastated. What people did not realize is that she was not devastated that he cheated. She was devastated that she was trapped with him. She spent a few days with friends and desperately did not want to return home. She wanted the relationship to be over, but she had no income to provide for herself. Her parents had told her all that she could not accomplish. They did not encourage her for all that she could accomplish. Therefore, she believed little in herself regarding what she could accomplish. She did not believe she could work a full-time job and maintain good grades in college. Spending her entire childhood watching her mom being trapped in a marriage in which she was miserable, Sidonie had been determined to never be in such a situation herself. There she was, trapped in a situation she did not want to be in. The relationship lasted a few more months before it officially ended, although it had already been over for a couple of months. It ended with his attempt to hit her. Since she was a very young child, Sidonie had been determined that no guy would ever be allowed to hit her as her mom had been hit. She would defend herself and there would not be a second opportunity. She defended herself and there was not a second opportunity for Benoni.

Sidonie was relieved that it was over with Benoni. She did not like him. She did not hate him. She had absolutely no feelings for him. She simply wanted him out of her life as if he had never entered it. However, she was grieving the loss of the relationship. She had built a life with someone losing her identity in her efforts to make the relationship successful, and now she had to adjust to being single and alone again without knowing who she was. She was completely lost now.

During the couple of weeks following the breakup, Sidonie contacted Damas to ask what was wrong with her. All her relationships had failed regardless of all her effort and all that she gave of herself. She had not yet realized that those relationships ended because she and those guys were simply not right for each other. Relationships ending allows the opportunity to find the right one. Damas sympathetically told her that it was not her, it was him. She was not been the problem, he had.

That conversation between Sidonie and Damas was discussed in a conversation between Sidonie and her mom. Her mom explained that Damas had been disappointed in his own younger sister because of her infidelity in her marriage, so he had seen Sidonie as a younger sister and Sidonie mistakenly perceived it as something more. There it was. Sidonie received confirmation of what she already knew to be true. Her mom was always going to blame her for that relationship in which he pursued a much younger minor girl. That was also confirmation for Sidonie that her mom would have blamed her for everything else that had happened to her as well. She then told her mom the remainder of the conversation wherein Damas told her to call him again later. She did not as she knew he would attempt to see her again. She did not want that. A week later she learned he had been engaged for two weeks, which meant he had been engaged for a week when he attempted to begin something with Sidonie again. Although her mom did not verbally respond, Sidonie read her mom's face and determined that knowledge still did not change her mom's mind about him or the whole situation.

That was when Sidonie began to truly recognize that her mom had her own issues resulting in misconceptions. Sidonie knew Damas was never going to change regardless of who he was with, and she had definitely made the right decision to permanently end any type of relationship with him. She again had to deal with the loneliness in addition to the pain, but by that time, she was becoming numb. She was grieving her previous relationship and the person she no longer was, but she was not feeling the pain and loneliness as strongly. She struggled through her next semester of college. It was a very difficult time for her as she was again preyed upon during this vulnerable time.

Sidonie had come to know a guy who had many mutual friends and acquaintances with her. He had been in a three-year relationship with someone she also knew. She thought she could trust him. She was hanging out with this guy, who was older than her but not very much older, and a mutual friend one night. She was drinking an alcoholic beverage. Upon finishing that beverage, the guy insisted on buying her another. She did want because she did not want to become intoxicated. He bought her one anyway and not wanting to be unappreciative, she drank it. The three were riding around. Without warning to Sidonie, they stopped, and the mutual friend exited the car. She was confused as to why he exited the car. She watched him walk to his automobile and enter. She was now intoxicated, which slowed her thought process. She did not think quickly enough to ask why he exited the car or why he was leaving to possibly stop him or go with him. They drove off, separately. She did not want to be alone with this guy. She wondered if this was another scheme against her. It was fine for them to hang out, but not just the two of them alone. He had a girlfriend.

The guy drove to a pond on a friend's property away from the nearest road. They exited the car to hang out by the pond. Briefly after, she got ill from the alcohol. Immediately after being ill, the guy kissed her intimately. She thought it was very disgusting for him to kiss her immediately after vomiting. She did not even want to kiss him. He kissed her again. She pushed him away and demanded he take her home.

He would not. He instead spoke about wanting to be with her. She told him she would walk home. She knew it would be a long walk down the long road, then even farther down the highway, which could be very dangerous. She was willing to take that chance to get out of this situation. Her chances of being raped walking down the highway would at least be fifty percent. Staying in this situation felt like a guarantee. Sidonie began walking in the direction from which they drove to the pond. She did not get far when she looked around and realized she was unable to see any type of path leading to the road. All she could see beyond the opening was trees. She had no idea which direction to take to the road and knew there were coyotes in the area. She turned around, adamantly walked directly to his car, opened the door demanding he take her home, then sat inside. He followed her still attempting to be with her, laid the seat back, and climbed on top of her. She continued to demand he take her home as she attempted to push him off. He would not stop. He continued as she repeatedly told him no. In her intoxicated weakness, she eventually ceased her failing attempts to stop him and lay there motionless waiting for it to be over. As if that was not bad enough, he told her afterwards that her body worked correctly with the correct responses. Sidonie was very disturbed by that statement. All she could think upon hearing that was that she did nothing. She did not move or participate in any way. There was absolutely no pleasure for her, only discomfort. She pondered how he could say that. Having gotten what he wanted from Sidonie, he finally took her home.

Devasted, she called Jacques at work the next day and told him she needed to speak with him. He told her the time he would have his lunch break for her to meet him. Sidonie cried as she confided in him what had occurred that night before. He was understanding and comforting. He also gave her some beneficial insight and advice as he noticed her blaming herself some for the incident. He told her she was too hard on herself. He also told her everyone makes mistakes, and most people made more serious and consequential mistakes than she did. That strongly resonated with her. He was correct. She had always been very judgmental and harshly critical of herself, more than she was of others. She felt that she was not allowed to make any mistake. She then realized that she was only human and could not possibly reach perfection regardless of her efforts. She also realized that mistakes could be opportunities to learn. This situation was not her mistake, other than trusting the wrong person, but those situations that were her mistakes were not very bad and did not make her a bad person. Jacques really knew her and knew she was a genuinely good person. That moment altered her perception of herself permanently and positively. She will forever be grateful to him for that. She felt somewhat better when she left him.

She had the displeasure of seeing that guy again one week later. He actually attempted to be with her again. He obviously did not realize what he had done to her. He perceived it as consensual. This time, she was completely sober. She made it very clear to him that she wanted nothing to do with him. He did not want to accept that. He attempted to make her feel bad for him in his desperation to be with her, but his attempt failed. He could not take advantage of her in that way again. He never had another opportunity. She was able to avoid being in his presence in the future.

One week later which was two weeks after that sexual assault, Sidonie was hanging out with her older distant relative with whom she was now living. She rode with that relative that night. While at the bar, her relative left with a man, leaving Sidonie stranded for a long time. It had gotten late, and she needed a ride. With her relative not having returned for her, Sidonie knew her relative was still with the man at her home. She did not want to go home until he was gone as he was a stranger to both of them. The best friend of Sidonie's first cousin was there and had been hanging out with her. He offered her a ride and to hang out at his house for a while before returning to her home. She had come to know this man well and did not believe she had any reason for concern because he would never do any wrong to his best friend's cousin. It was a code among friends of her family. She was wrong again.

Sidonie had been drinking. This man, who was much older than her, had bought her a strong drink earlier. This situation was very similar to the prior one. She attempted to push him off without the strength to fight. She repeatedly told him no, but he disregarded her words. She again eventually ceased her failing attempts to stop him and lay there motionless waiting for it to be over. He then took her home. Sidonie was devastated once again. He also did not seem to realize what he had done to her and perceived it as consensual. Did they not know what rape was? Did they think that because they did not beat her, or she did not hit them that it was not rape? Sidonie was a very petite girl, barely five feet tall. These men were tall and heavy men, not boys. Had they forgotten what the word "no" means, a word they had learned as toddlers? How many times does it take to say "no" for them to accept it? She had even attempted to walk home to not be intimate with one of them. How was that not a clear indication that she did not want to be with him? Why her? Did they recognize her vulnerability with all her trauma, of which they could not have known, and see her as weak and easy prey? She was still dealing with such abuse from her childhood. When would it stop? Most people considered her to be attractive with a good personality. People of many types seemed to enjoy her company. They liked hanging out with her, but she was no more special than anyone else. Why did these guys want to be with her to the extent that they would force it? They each took something very personal and very special from her that she did not want to share with them. She had not shared that with many and was selective in doing so based on her feelings and emotional connection. She did not connect with them in that way and did not have those types of feelings for them. She did not love them like that. Perhaps they perceived it as they were very good at tempting her and had been able to convince her to change her mind, which was not the case. That would be delusional. She had not been tempted to be with either of them. She continued to ponder these questions for many years to come. It was like a jungle out in the world as she struggled to recognize predators and develop the skills to avoid them and protect herself from them. She was too trusting for this world.

Again, she contacted Jacques the next day and met with him. He gave her more beneficial advice as she cried on his shoulder. He told her that alcohol was the problem and she needed to stop drinking. She carefully processed that advice and realized that it was not necessarily alcohol as she had never been in such a weakened state from drinking regular alcoholic beverages. She had been quite responsible with her drinking in the past. Each one of these situations, including the one with her cousin, involved highly potent alcohol. She was not able to control that as well because it would have much more of an effect on her very quickly. She had never drunk alcohol regularly, only when hanging out with people. Even then, sometimes she would not drink at all. She decided to avoid all alcoholic beverages of high potency. That worked for her as she went forward with her life. Sidonie was never sexually assaulted again, but those incidents made her bitter. She became bitter toward all guys she did not already know who attempted to speak with her.

Sidonie never told anyone besides Jacques about those two incidents. She feared that some people, especially guys, would not consider those situations to be a violation against her, but she undoubtedly knew it was. She could not deal with anything negative people might say about her regarding those situations. She was still struggling to deal with the pain from her other traumas, including her childhood sexual abuse.

Sidonie developed the skills to be successfully vindictive to people. Some deserved it, but Sidonie did not want to be that type of person. She preferred to directly confront people with any issue she felt needed to be delt with and potentially resolved. However, she did practice some vindictive behavior with a couple of players who were very persistent with her despite her bitterness. They would not quit pursuing her. Sidonie decided that if they were that desperate to play their game, she would play. She had learned from the best and knew she would not lose. They were begging for it and deserved it. She inconvenienced them and had them do ridiculous things for her to humiliate themselves. She did this without giving anything in return. Eventually, they decided they wanted no more of that and retreated in defeat. That was how Sidonie got players to leave her alone.

Sidonie's intimate virtue was very special to her, almost sacred. Because of that, she felt as though she, in a sense, belonged to a guy after being intimate with him and felt obligated to have a relationship with him. That may have played a role in her remaining in relationships longer than she should have. Sadly, she felt that way with the much older man after what he did to her as he relentlessly pursued her. She did not feel that way with the previous guy because he was committed to someone at the time and Sidonie felt that, in a sense, they already belonged to each other. Her issues from her childhood were so extensive that this was how messed up she was. Because of her mom's demented perceptions, she believed guys were never completely in the wrong and nothing was ever as bad as it seemed to Sidonie. Her mom had always made it seem as though Sidonie made things seem worse than they were, even though she rarely made an issue of anything. At some point, Sidonie began spending time with this man and his friends, sometimes spending time with only him and a couple who were in a relationship. It seemed to be like a relationship but was actually not to her. She really did not want a relationship with him, only a friendship and her desire for that was limited. He wanted a relationship with her. He applied much effort to earning her affection. He catered to her. Sidonie eventually agreed to progress into a relationship with him for a few months. She was intimate with him one more time, consensually. She felt no such feelings for him. She had given it a real chance, but she could not get over the circumstances of their initial intimacy and he was too old for her. It was not going to work. She was now able to move on. He seemed hurt by that. She was never alone with him again.

One evening, Sidonie and her friend's mother went to hang out at a local bar where she was friends with the employees. She always felt safe there as the employees always looked after her. She had a great time, except for the two guys who were wanting to leave with her. One she had met in high school and had family ties with. He knew Sidonie was not the type to have one-time intimate encounters. The other was a friend of the bartender's from out of town who went to work with him that one night because he was short of staff. Sidonie was repeatedly adamant with them both that no one was leaving with her except the woman who had gone with her. She thought they had finally accepted that.

The bar closed, but some customers were not ready to leave. The door was locked, and it was declared a private party, which made it legal for them to stay. Sidonie decided to dance on the bar. She had never done anything to intentionally draw attention to herself. She was proud of herself for having the confidence to do that. Her bartender friend was concerned that she might hit her head on the fans above the bar, so she was carried to the pool table. Sidonie found that amusing as he must not have realized how very short she was. Sidonie continued to dance on the pool table. She was not dressed provocatively. Her body was fully covered by her outfit. She also did not dance seductively. She considered those things before climbing onto the bar. She was having innocent fun.

Maybe that was the innocence others still saw in her. She did not perceive dancing anywhere as provocative or seductive if the dancing was not seductive. It was just dancing.

Eventually, everyone was ready to leave. Sidonie and the woman who went with her walked to Sidonie's car. The guy Sidonie had already known followed her. He attempted to change her mind regarding him leaving with her, something he was not going to achieve. Sidonie sat in her car as he stooped beside so she could not close the door and leave. As he persisted in changing her mind, they heard a voice. They both looked in the direction of that voice to see the other guy who had also wanted to leave with her. He was standing at a distance. As they looked at him, he was holding a shiny, silver pistol with a pearl handle pointed directly at the guy stooped beside Sidonie. In addition to this action, his words expressed his determination not to allow the other guy to leave with her. The two were in shock. Sidonie quickly realized that if he pulled the trigger, he would likely shoot the guy beside her. If he missed, he would likely shoot Sidonie as she was behind the guy in the direct path of the gun. If he were to miss both, he might shoot the woman in the car with her as she was also in the direct path of the gun behind Sidonie. Her shock left no room for any other emotions. She was in disbelief that she might witness someone be murdered beside her or be murdered herself. Her bartender friend was taking out the trash at that time. He was also in shock upon seeing the pistol. He walked toward the guy holding it attempting to convince that guy to give the pistol to him. After a bit of coaxing, the guy gave it to the bartender. Sidonie then knew they were all safe. The guy went back into the bar as instructed by the bartender.

The bartender friend profusely apologized to Sidonie. She knew it was not his fault and informed him of that. He would have never allowed anyone suspected of less aggressive behavior around. The other guy beside her immediately walked away and left. Perhaps he no longer thought his attempts were worth the effort. That was the greatest fear for her life Sidonie has experienced. She left still in shock and confused about how she felt or should feel about the situation that had just occurred. The next time Sidonie saw her bartender friend, he continued to apologize, although she expressed to him that he had no fault in the matter. He explained that he had no idea that guy would ever do something like that. He had no idea he had a gun with him, and he was not allowed there ever again.

Mutual friends of Sidonie and Benoni were always sharing with her what was going on in his life, even though she had informed them she did not want to know. She genuinely did not care and wanted to move on, but they were not allowing her to do so by continuing to share such information with her. Camille had gotten married and moved to another state during Sidonie's relationship with Benoni. She insisted Sidonie spend the summer with them. Sidonia needed to get away, so she left immediately following the end of the semester. The moment she drove onto the main street of that city with all her belongings, she felt a huge weight lifted from her. She had not realized until that moment the weight of expectations she had always felt upon her. She had always felt that she was under a microscope with everyone waiting for her to make a mistake they could use to declare her a bad person. She had girls attempt to do that to her in the past. The people who were the worst at accusing her of doing wrongs were her mom and brother. Unlike other people, they did not tell such things to others, but they were definitely harsh with Sidnie in their accusations. Now, she was somewhere that only two people knew her. There were no expectations of her from people there; therefore, no pressure of expectations. She could be whatever version of herself she chose without worrying about the slightest missteps. She felt freer than ever.

Chapter 4

Over the summer, Sidonie overcame all the past abuse and reached a point of forgiveness for her parents and brother. She no longer felt dirty, worthless, or like damaged goods. She imagined what her parents' childhoods must have been like for them and developed a deep understanding and compassion for them as she realized their issues. She came to understand that their abusiveness was not personal against her or the other immediate family members specifically. Not knowing how to deal with their issues, their immediate family members were the ones they could project their negative emotions onto without losing them, especially with the children having no option to leave that environment when they were minors. Sidonie had finally begun to acquire a positive self-image.

However, the accumulation of emotional pain from everything else that had been occurring in her adult life, in addition to that from her childhood, had become unbearable in combination with the loneliness. She had been able to relieve the loneliness with relationships, but between those relationships, she suffered both. Enduring only the pain was bearable, but the combination of both no longer was. Her brain must have had a mechanism of self-preservation because she entered a period of emotional numbness. She became completely numb to all emotions. She had felt so much so deeply for so long that she now felt nothing; nothing except a slight, lingering sadness. It was a relief to no longer feel pain.

As the end of the summer approached, Sidonie decided to stay and enroll in college there. She did not want to go back to her hometown area. She was better where she was now living. Much to her surprise, she received a call from the guy from the pond. She had no idea how he had gotten her phone number until he informed her that he had seen her parents somewhere and got it from her mom. She could not understand why her mom gave him her number. Her mom barely knew him and had no idea the circumstances of their acquaintance. In the conversation, he claimed his girlfriend had been unfaithful, then had been spending the summer out of state. For confirmation of the type of person she already knew him to be, Sidonie asked if the relationship had ended. He simply repeated the circumstances and never answered the question she asked. He was attempting to establish an unwanted relationship with Sidonie while still technically in a relationship with someone else. She was correct about him, not that it would have made any difference to her considering what he had done. He eagerly inquired when she would be returning as though he still believed he had a chance to be with Sidonie. She informed him that she had decided to continue living where she was and would not be returning. It worked perfectly for her. She did not want to deal with him anymore and would not have to encounter him anywhere at that distance from her hometown. That was the last time he made any attempt with her.

Later that same day, she spoke with her mom who was concerned about the guy's eagerness to contact her. Not even knowing what had occurred, her mom was not fond of the idea of Sidonie being with that guy. Sidonie inquired with frustration as to why her mom gave him her number. Her mom did not directly answer her question either.

After months of emotional numbness, it was no longer a relief to not feel pain. When Sidonie looked into a mirror, she would only see an empty shell. It was as though there was no soul inside of her body. She was not living, only existing. That was the worst feeling she ever experienced. She would have cried but had no emotions to do so. With the excessive number of tears she had cried throughout her life, it was strange to not be able to shed any. She had a break from that also. The sadness may have been grief. Sidonie was grieving that young child and that teenager who had once resided within her body. She grieved for that young child's innocence she never had. She internally wept over that young child's suffering and that teenager's consuming loneliness. She thought they were gone, but she now felt them. She felt them hidden in the depths of the cold, dark, desolate space with which she was too familiar. She comforted them and assured them none of it was their fault and they did not deserve any of it. She assured them they were genuinely good and always had been. Then, Sidonie was able to bring light into them, rescuing them from the darkness. They remained nestled in the comfort of warm, healing light for some years after, then she felt them no more.

Sidonie found a roommate who she worked with, and they rented an apartment together. During this time, a new friend of Sidonie's encouraged her to date a guy who was very interested in Sidonie, but she was not very interested in him. It was brief. He was not her type. There were a few other guys in the area where Sidonie now resided who were very interested in her and wanted to date her. She really enjoyed their company, but she did not have the same feelings for them. She did not typically waste her time dating guys with whom she felt no such emotional connection. She spent time with them as friends, but that connection was not something she could create. It either existed or it did not.

Sidonie met the family of her new roommate, Musetta. They had a rule that once their children moved out of their home, they were never allowed to move back. Circumstances became concerning with Musetta. Musetta had only had one friend throughout high school and after. Briefly after becoming roommates, she seemed to no longer want to spend time with that friend. She only wanted to spend time with Sidonie. Musetta attempted to assert herself into every situation with Sidonie and any guy who expressed interest in Sidonie. She got upset with Sidonie when Sidonie hung out with others in which Musetta was not included. She also seemed to want only the two of them spending time together with no one else. Musetta once left Sidonie stranded at a nightclub while taking a guy home with her because Sidonie was socializing with others and not focused on Musetta. Sidonie was able to get a ride home, but her purse with her keys were locked in Musetta's automobile. The music was playing very loudly in the apartment. Musetta would not answer their door, either because she could not hear Sidonie knocking on the door, or she was punishing Sidonie. Fortunately, Sidonie was able to find somewhere safe to sleep that night. She had expanded her social life there as well.

One of the guys who had been interested in Sidonie eventually decided to move on to another girl. He and Sidonie had been hanging out together as good friends. They got along well, but she had no romantic interest in him, so she had no problem with him seeing someone else. However, others believed she should, including Musetta. Regardless of the number of times Sidonie expressed that it did not bother her, some people still believed it did.

One evening Musetta initiated a conversation about the matter. Sidonie engaged in fun. She genuinely had no problem with that guy seeing the new girl. She had been friendly with the girl and had even hung out with her some. The girl had begun to unintentionally irritate Sidonie for some reason. Perhaps she also believed Sidonie was bothered by her new relationship and had unintentional behavior toward Sidonie. Things had gotten somewhat awkward between them, but Sidonie felt that it was because of the pressure of others making an issue about the situation. Sidonie honestly wanted to simply be friends with both the girl and the guy.

In the conversation with Musetta that evening, Sidonie jokingly agreed with her about getting revenge on the girl. Musetta suggested that Sidonie slash the girl's tire on her car. Sidonie went along with that idea in the conversation. The two girls were laughing in amusement. The conversation was not a serious one. Sidonie had similar conversations with friends in the past. Those conversations were only for amusement with no one involved being serious or attempting to act on any malicious behavior discussed. Sidonie genuinely believed this conversation was the same, until Musetta insisted they go slash the girl's tire then with it now dark outside. Sidonie was surprised by that but still believed that Musetta would not actually participate in such an action. Sidonie was definitely not going to slash that girl's tire. She felt no ill intention toward the girl to do anything harmful or mean to her, and she would not slash her tire if she did. Musetta expressed to Sidonie her loyalty indicating that she would not allow anyone to do Sidonie wrong without suffering consequences. That was not the type of friend Sidonie wanted. She did not want harm or meanness to others on her behalf. She had better ways of dealing with situations in which she was wronged. They were to pretend those wrongs did not affect her and move on as if those people, who had wronged her, were insignificant to her with no power to affect her life. That was the best revenge for Sidonie as she knew very well what feeling insignificant was like. Musetta persisted, although Sidonie attempted to convince her there was no reason to do such a thing. Sidonie eventually succumbed to Musetta's persistence and left with her. Sidonie still did not believe Musetta would actually encourage Sidonie in such behavior or commit such an action herself. Sidonie was expecting Musetta to begin to reconsider as they neared the girl's residence. They would both agree to not do it and go home. That did not happen. Musetta was a different type of person than Sidonie was familiar with.

As they were approaching the girl's car, Sidonie again began to attempt to convince Musetta that they should not do anything to the girl's car. She declared that the girl did not deserve it. Musetta was determined. She parked behind the girl's car, took out a knife, and encouraged Sidonie to slash the girl's tire. Sidonie continued in her attempt to convince her that it was not worth it. There were no benefits to damaging the girl's property. Musetta became angry with Sidonie and accused her of being weak for not following through. Sidonie was never serious about any of it and had not thought Musetta was either, until now. Sidonie refused to participate in any way. She remained in the car as Musetta declared that she would do it herself and exited the car. She walked to the girl's car and jabbed the knife into the tire. Sidonie was sickened by that. The girl was a good person and did not deserve any bad. Sidonie realized in that moment that Musetta was not very stable, and she should not participate in any adventures with her or any conversations of such.

As news of the incident spread, some people assumed Sidonie was the one who had slashed the tire. She wondered if Musetta had perhaps said anything to anyone to indicate that possibility. The people in that area had known Sidonie for only a number of months, but did they really think she would do something like that? Did they really believe she was vengeful? She was honest each time she denied doing that but knew her claim did not eliminate the suspicion. The girl had reported the incident to the police. Sidonie was not one to tell of another person's wrongdoing without specifically being asked. That was not how she was raised, nor were most people from her hometown area. She would not have answered any questions with lies, she simply would not volunteer information. Had the police questioned her asking if she knew who slashed the tire, she would have told them the truth of the whole situation. Although, Sidonie had concerns that if she had told anyone that it was Musetta who slashed the tire, Musetta may have lied, declaring that Sidonie had done it. Sidonie was also aware that she could have been considered an accomplice even though she attempted to prevent it. She was not brave enough to physically get in Musetta's way with a knife in her hand in an attempt to stop her. That was a side of Musetta that Sidonie had not seen. The police never spoke with Sidonie.

The final behavior that prompted Sidonie to break her lease occurred when she was dating the one guy she dated there. He was working late and informed Sidonie that he would call her when his shift ended. Sidonie informed Musetta that he would be calling late. This would not be his first time calling late. The apartment in which they lived had one large bedroom. They shared the bedroom with each their own bed. The telephone was next to Musetta's bed. Musetta had never had an issue with anyone calling late. When Sidonie awoke the next morning, she immediately realized her boyfriend had not called. She looked at the telephone and noticed it was removed from the base. The call could not have been received. At that time Musetta was beginning to wake up. Sidonie inquired as to why the telephone was removed from the base. Musetta claimed that she had removed it so their sleep would not be disturbed. She had not done such a thing before. As they climbed out of bed to prepare for their day, Sidonie noticed Musetta remove a large kitchen knife from underneath her pillow. That seriously concerned Sidonie. That was also a new behavior. She inquired as to why she had the knife under her pillow. Musetta claimed she felt unsafe as someone could have entered their bedroom through the balcony window. Musetta had not had that concern previously. Sidonie felt unsafe at this point. She may have been overreacting, but she knew the dangers in the human jungle.

In the past, she had believed that certain things could not happen to her as had happened to others shown in news reports or true story programs and movies. Most people she knew also thought the same about themselves and people they knew. Too much had happened to Sidonie to believe that now. She knew that whatever happened to anyone, could also happen to her. Musetta had been displaying unusual behavior that was becoming concerning to Sidonie. She seemed to become somewhat possessive of Sidonie, wanting Sidonie to only spend time with her. Sidonie considered that Musetta may have had the knife to threaten Sidonie had she awoke in the night and attempted to place the telephone on the base to prevent Sidonie from speaking with her boyfriend.

This scenario was not only from Sidonie's observation. She had been sensing negative vibes from Musetta in certain concerning situations. Sidonie immediately felt strong negative vibes in this situation. Whatever Musetta's true reasons for such actions, they were not of good intentions. Sidonie considered that Musetta might be somewhat psychotic. She was not going to risk remaining in what she now felt to be a potentially dangerous situation. She made arrangements with Camille and her husband to temporarily live with them again and broke her lease.

Musetta was very upset as she could not afford the full rent and utility bills herself and could not return to her parents' home to reside. Although she expressed her desire to remain friends with Sidonie, she informed Sidonie that she had spoken with the manager of the apartment complex who explained the only option for Musetta was to take legal action against Sidonie. This would have cost Musetta approximately the same amount as Sidonie's half of the remaining lease or more. Musetta's older brother agreed to become her roommate to help her. Sidonie believed that to be the best thing for Musetta. Her family were good people, and her brother could have helped her become stable, or he could have at least become aware she may have needed other help. Her family definitely needed to know some of Musetta's behaviors. This is how they would become aware as they probably would not have believed Sidonie had she informed them. Sidonie was free and safe. She was never pursued for any responsibility to that lease or any accountability for the tire.

When she was finally able to feel again months later, the first emotion Sidonie felt was the one most familiar to her, pain. That emotion was different, though. It was not the same debilitating pain accompanied by anguish. Regardless, she was surprised by the fact that she was happy to feel pain again. She was simply happy to feel any emotion because she felt alive again. She believed that period of emotional numbness allowed her to heal from all her suffering throughout her life. She was renewed. She healed the young child and the teenager then, it was like a rebirth of a stronger, healthier version of herself. For the first time in her life, she loved herself. She respected, appreciated, and even admired herself. She admired herself for all that she had overcome and doing so without self-destructing. She had triumphed! She had never thought it at all possible for her to ever feel so positively about herself. She did not need anyone to love or validate her as she could adequately do that herself. She was able to give herself everything she needed. Everyone else was a bonus, but not a necessity. That is when she began to flourish. She was ready to conquer the world.

Approximately the middle of the semester, Sidonie began missing Chrétien. His relationship had ended shortly after Sidonie's relationship with Benoni ended. She loved living there, but she was really missing Chrétien and needed to see once more if there could possibly be something substantial between them. As the end of the semester approached, she made plans to move back to her hometown.

Within two weeks of moving back, Sidonie knew she would not last living there for a year. That place was not for her. She would not flourish well there. During those first couple of months of her return was when she recognized her mom's treatment of her as psychological abuse. It only occurred once every couple of months from that time forward. She would eventually have to transfer elsewhere for college anyway, so she planned to transfer early. She was not yet sure exactly when.

Sidonie became aware that Chrétien had a new girlfriend. A few weeks later, she saw him. As always, he greeted her with a hug. The hug was very brief as he was in a hurry. His interactions with her had never been that brief. As he rushed off, she called his name. He looked back but continued to his destination telling her he had to go. She had wanted to tell him she missed him. In that moment, she knew a relationship between them would never be. She knew she had to close that chapter of her life permanently and move on.

Sidonie turned twenty-one years old and felt that she had completed her process of dealing with and healing from all her traumas and had overcome all her issues resulting from them. For the previous couple of years, everyone in her life, aside from her immediate family, had wanted to spend time with her, confided in her, trusted her, and enjoyed her company as she was being her authentic self. Because of that, Sidonie finally began to perceive herself as normal, good, not stupid, and having common sense. She had earned her positive, stellar reputation by working very hard to become the best version of herself and allowing people to really know the person she was. The revelation that there was not anything wrong with her was empowering. She had been pretending to have confidence, but now she actually did. She also realized the strength she had to be able to get through it all triumphantly and able to flourish. She knew that she could get through anything and be okay.

She had always remained true to herself and was always genuine with others. She was very strong in her individuality, but she had also always worked extremely hard to hide her traumas, issues, and emotions from everyone. She did not want to be perceived as weak, vulnerable, or pathetic and treated accordingly. Her parents made Sidonie and her brother particularly good actors by demanding they always hide all the abuse within their home and pretend that everything was fine. The consequences of not doing so were more than they felt capable of enduring. Sidonie no longer had those consequential issues from abuse to hide. They were resolved. She could finally live freely without hiding any part of herself. With all the self-analyzing Sidonie had done throughout her life, she knew herself better than anyone. She knew what she needed, wanted, and what worked best for her. She knew what she did not need, did not want, and what did not work for her. She knew how to deal with matters in ways that were effective for her. She would never again allow anyone to determine these things for her. For the first time in her life, she could realistically see a future. She was able to set goals and believed that she could achieve them. Closing that chapter with Chrétien provided more clarity for her future as he was no longer an unknown factor. With all these positive changes in Sidonie's perception of herself, the type of guys she had been interested in changed to an interest in a better type as she now felt worthy of better.

Sidonie realized she was comfortable single. She

also realized that although she had loved her boyfriends to varying degrees, she had never been in love with any of them. She did not want a relationship with anyone at that point. She wanted to enjoy her life without having to consider someone else in her decisions. She set her goals to build a life for herself by herself. Sidonie could no longer imagine ever settling down with anyone. She could see casually dating, but never getting serious with anyone. She believed she could not rely on anyone to always be there for her in the way she needed. She had learned the hard way that she was the only person who she could truly rely on for that. She also had not had the proper examples and teachings of marriage or parenting from her parents. She knew those roles would be extremely challenging for her. She did not want to put anyone through that with her or damage her children as her parents had damaged her and her brother.

Sidonie was anticipating moving away to a new area where no one knew her as she made her final plans of where and which semester she would transfer. She knew she would make her way in life wherever she went. She had learned that while living in a different state. She would always make friends and she would always have one or two of them bring her into their family, providing her with people who were like family between visits with her own family.

Sidonie knew the life she wanted to build. As she set her goals, made her plans, and executed them, her life continued evolving. She met someone one year older than her through mutual friends. They became very good friends. They were becoming best friends when they began a relationship. This relationship was different. It felt natural and was easy. She did not need to work hard at this relationship as she had in past relationships. It was not complicated and nurtured her inner peace. This guy nurtured her in all aspects with the freedom for her to simply be herself. They were on the same level intellectually, had the same main goals in life, and understood each other. They enjoyed each other's company and connected on a very deep level. This was a love she had never experienced. It was very fulfilling. He loved her in a way that convinced her she was not meant to live her life alone. She married that guy and built a beautiful life with him. Timing was everything. Had Sidonie not overcome and healed from her trauma to become this person she now was, this relationship would have never worked. No relationship would have. God had gotten her to where she needed to be.

Prior to her relationship with her husband, Sidonie had another guy attempt to date her. They worked at the same place of business. He noticed her during one of their shifts and went to speak with her. After the introduction, he inquired more into who she was. She recognized his name from her brother speaking of him in the past. He had been friends with her brother. They had often hung out together during her brother's wild, popular days. She informed him who her brother was. He confirmed in excitement that he and her brother had been friends. He seemed to think that was in his favor with her. On the contrary, that was a warning for her. She no longer had any interest in that type of guy. However, she agreed to go for a ride with him after work. She was quite sure he knew her brother well enough to know the consequences if he were to harm or even attempt to harm his little sister in any manner as he was still protective of her, so she felt safe.

He was very proud of the car he drove and seemed to expect Sidonie to be impressed. She was not. Sidonie had never been a materialistic or high maintenance person. She had no desire to be. She was more practical and genuine. She did not perceive material belongings as an indication of the type of person someone was. One's behavior and the manner in which one treats others has always determined that for Sidonie. They engaged in conversation to become more acquainted, but nothing more. He did not attempt even a kiss. She was relieved and felt very respected, however, she had no interest in him beyond that of a friend.

A few weeks later, they crossed paths hanging out at the same place. He decided to go to the next place Sidonie was going, obviously to spend time with her. They rode separately in each their own automobile. Sidonie did not ignore him but spent little time with him. She remained on the dance floor most of the time as usual while he remained at the bar the entire time. They greeted each other in passing at work, which was seldom. She was a hugger, so she had probably hugged him a time or two but never anything more. She had never even held his hand or given him a simple kiss on his cheek, nor he to her. There had never been anything romantic between them, although she knew that was what he wanted. They had not spoken since prior to the beginning of her new relationship.

In the months approaching her wedding, Sidonie received a phone call from a guy who was currently living in another state, and she had known well for many years. He had claimed to be in love with her many months prior. When she told him she was getting married and was pregnant, he asked her if that was what she really wanted. She assured him that it was. The tone of his voice immediately changed from happy and excited to speak with her to disappointed and hurt. She knew he was very upset about her committing to someone else for the rest of her life.

One night while hanging out, she saw two guys who she had been friends with since high school. They both begged her not to marry her fiancé. Early in the week of her wedding, Sidonie went to her place of employment to collect her pay. She had just worked her final shift there the evening prior. It was almost time for shift change as the guy who had been friends with her brother arrived and prepared to begin his shift. During that time, he heard some of the other employees congratulating Sidonie on her upcoming wedding. As she was going to walk passed him, he began speaking to her somewhat stern. He was seeking confirmation of what he had heard. She confirmed that she was getting married and informed him that she was pregnant. He instantly became very angry with her about the fact that she was getting married. He was obviously still very interested in a relationship with her. She was surprised by that because he had not made much effort to pursue her, and they had not spoken in many months. Sidonie determined he must have assumed she was not ready for a relationship, so he would wait until she was to pursue another attempt with her.

Sidonie could not understand the fact that while all these guys were upset about her getting married, the fact that she was pregnant did not seem to be of any significance to them. They only made reference to her getting married, never the fact that she was going to have a baby. It seemed they still wanted an opportunity with her even though she was having a baby with someone else. Sidonie could not comprehend any of them wanting her with someone else's child. She had not had any idea that her two friends from high school had ever had such an interest in her. She obviously had no radar to detect such interest. Another had been informing her of conversations he had overheard at different times in which different guys were discussing the fact that Sidonie was getting married. According to him, these guys were upset about that. This was all very shocking to Sidonie. She was simply her, no one extra special. She could not believe that she was someone who many guys would have that type of interest in, especially that many and the type of decent guys many of them were with no ingenuine motive. She had spent most of her life believing she was insignificant, worthless, useless, and a nobody whom no decent guy would ever want. Now there were many guys upset about losing any future opportunity of a relationship with her for the potential of building a life together.

As Sidonie was preparing for her upcoming wedding, she was packing her things to move in with her new husband when she discovered her notebook of poetry. Being near it provided discomfort for her.

Even from a distance, she could feel all the pain, anguish, and loneliness expressed inside. She could feel the cold emptiness of that dark, desolate place in which she had spent much of her life. She could feel the weight of the burdens in it. Sidonie could not have it near her, so she threw it away. She had always been a talented creative writer. Many years later she wished she had kept it simply to see how good her poetry actually was from a lighter and more mature perspective.

Briefly after getting married, Sidonie began having guys, as she crossed paths with them, asking to be placed on her list. She had no idea what list the first guy was referring to. When she inquired, he informed her that he was referring to the list of guys as prospects for a relationship in the event her marriage failed. Sidonie had never heard of such a list and had no idea there would be enough guys interested in her to need to create one. This request continued throughout the first years of her marriage becoming fewer and farther between. A couple of guys requested to be placed at the top of the list. The last request was at least eight years into her marriage. She had three children then and had forgotten most of the guys who had made that request in those previous years as she had never kept a written record. It was unbelievable to Sidonie that guys still wanted an opportunity with her knowing she had a child with someone else, then two, and now three children. She will never understand that. It will always seem unrealistic to her. She became far more significant than she had ever considered possible. She must have been quite amazing, but she still could not see herself as any more amazing than the next person.

Three years into her marriage and pregnant with her second child, Sidonie and her second boyfriend crossed paths. He expressed to her that he wished the child she was carrying was his. She felt sad for him. He had not had the opportunity to begin his own family with someone who was right for him as he had wanted for many years. Now, Sidonie had begun her family with someone else and was expanding it. Throughout the years since, he has expressed his deep feelings for her without stating so or crossing any boundaries. He has never attempted anything inappropriate with her, insinuated she leave her husband, or anything of the sort. He has respected her, her husband, and her marriage. He has not been the only one. A couple of others have done the same. She has remained friends with them all on the rare occasions in which she is unintentionally at the same location at the same time as them. Sidonie has felt sad for them, but she is only one person and can only devote herself completely to one person. She understands that we cannot control such feelings for others and is compassionate about that. However, we can control our actions. One crossed that boundary. Sidonie did not allow that. She no longer associates with him in any way.

Four years into her marriage now with two children, a mutual friend of Sidonie and her husband went to their home to speak with Sidonie, knowing her husband would not be there at that time. She and this guy had briefly dated for two weeks sometime prior to her meeting her husband. Sidonie was grateful that her mother-in-law was there so as not to have any suspicions from anyone of anything inappropriate. He insisted on speaking outside. In that conversation, he expressed regrets and indicated those regrets were regarding Sidonie. He asked her if she believed she could spend the rest of her life with only her husband. Sidonie confirmed that she could and meant it. She was very happy with her husband and very in love with him. She definitely wanted to spend the remainder of her life with him. Four or five years later, she crossed paths with this guy again. In their conversation, he explained to her that her being married was very difficult for him. He seemed somewhat angry while expressing this. His anger seemed to be his expression of being upset and hurt over her not being with him. Sidonie had not had any idea this guy ever had strong feelings such as those for her. He had not indicated such in all the years of their friendship. Like all the others, he had his opportunity when she was single. He had his opportunity when they dated but chose to break up with her. Perhaps all those guys who had that interest in her had assumed that she was not ready for a serious relationship. Perhaps some of them were not ready themselves and assumed they would have more time for that opportunity with Sidonie. Her husband had not been willing to take that chance and risk being in the same situation as this guy and others with the regret of having lost that opportunity without having attempted when that opportunity existed.

Sidonie had been relieved to be out of the jungle of unmarried life. She felt that her husband had rescued her from that unpredictable, insecure life in which she was always attempting to evade predators. She has not wanted to reenter that confusing jungle of struggle.

Sidonie had always had people in her life who did not believe that situations were as she explained them to be. Her mom had always thought Sidonie overreacted to situations making them seem more serious than they were. Beginning in her teens and into her adult life, she also had a couple of friends who seemed to think the same about a couple of certain situations involving Sidonie. There were situations that Sidonie knew had her friends not witnessed, they would not have believed they actually occurred, or at least not to the extent or manner in which they occurred. They did not believe such things could happen to Sidonie or anyone they knew. Sidonie also had difficulty believing some of these situations had happened to her. Some of these things were only seen on television. They did not actually occur to individuals who were known to Sidonie, or individuals known to anyone in her life. It was much more unbelievable when considering all those situations had happened to that one particular individual. She had always found it to be insane that she was that one particular individual who had experienced it all.

Sidonie had really lived. She had suffered many traumas and difficulties, but she had an exciting life and many great moments. Those are the memories which she most reminisces. There were moments in which she lived on the edge some, but she always had the self-conviction and self-control not to step off the edge and to bring herself back from the edge. That was where the exciting experiences were without regret, guilt, or significant consequences. When she had her first child, she was ready to make her life about her child and future children. She had her time to live on her terms, now it was her children's time for the fun and excitement of life and all the opportunities life had to offer. She gave all of herself to her husband and children, providing her children with a good childhood filled with experiences, as well as protection to preserve their innocence, and preparing them to conquer the world on their own.

As Sidonie settled into marriage and began creating a family of her own, her mom began to gradually become more controlling over Sidonie and her life. She began very subtly and became less subtle over time. Her brother's life also evolved, but his was less stable. Eventually and without Sidonie realizing, they both reached the same level of psychological abusiveness they had inflicted upon Sidonie for all those many years in the past. However, it did not have the same effect on Sidonie, nor did it affect her to the extent it had before because she knew she was not the problem. They were projecting their own insecurities with themselves onto her without realizing. Neither of them had ever realized what they did to Sidonie and still did not. They have never seen anything wrong in their actions against her but, in contradiction, believed them to be beneficial for her. They seemed to think she still needed parenting after many years of success in marriage, parenting, and life in general. Although she still strongly defended herself to them each time, it was more difficult to abruptly leave those situations with her children. She attempted to protect her children from such behaviors by being subtle in dealing with these matters in their presence. The more she did against what her parents wanted, the more they attempted to control her and her life, something they had not been able to come close to doing since she had moved out of their home at the age of eighteen.

Around the age of twenty-six with five years of marriage and two children, Sidonie heard a conversation between her supervisor and a co-worker. That conversation was regarding dysfunction in their own families beginning in their childhoods. She made a comment indicating her personal knowledge of such dysfunction. She was very surprised by her supervisor's response as he seemed very surprised by her comment. He stated that he thought she had come from a perfect, religious family and had a perfect childhood. Without sharing details, she confirmed her comment and informed him that had definitely not been her situation. He had no idea the major compliment that was for Sidonie. She walked away from that conversation feeling completely accomplished. She had accomplished her first major goal in life. She had overcome all the dysfunction to become completely functional living a happy, virtuous, and productive life. His statement was confirmation that no one had any suspicions of her having had any trauma or dysfunction in her life because there was no longer any existing damage from any of it. She felt that she could relax as she no longer had to put forth the effort to become the person she wanted to be. She had truly become that person. She had come full circle. Without realizing at the time, all the effort she had made to improve all those unpleasant aspects of herself had resulted in her becoming the best version of herself. She had worked very hard to achieve this and was very proud that she had done that all herself. She was a self-made woman. No one deserved credit for the person she had become and the type of life she chose to live except her.

In her adult life, Sidonie never considered her parents in her decisions. She never made any decisions with intent to hurt or rebel against them. That would have been making decisions based on her parents, which would not have been beneficial to herself or anyone. She knew she did not want to live the life her parents had because it had been miserable for both of them. It became less miserable after their children were grown and on their own, leaving them with only each other at home, but they were still miserable. She was not going to live as they did to become miserable as they were. Sidonie made decisions based on what her own family and herself needed, what was best for them, and what worked for them. Her responsibility was to her own family and herself for the benefit of her own family, not her parents. Regardless, they seemed intent on gaining control of her and her life. There was only ever right or wrong with her parents and brother, no preference or opinion, and their way was always the only correct one. Sidonie determined that not living their way, not doing everything their way, and not making the decisions they would was perceived by them as a contradiction to them. Perhaps that contradiction disturbed them because it did not validate their parenting, spousal, and life skills when that contradiction was beneficial to Sidonie and her family, which it mostly was. Perhaps they needed Sidonie to prove them correct by failing with her contradictions or following their ways so they would not feel like failures themselves, which they would never admit. None of them would ever admit to any of their failures. Sidonie has been grateful to be different. Not acknowledging her own failures would have prevented her from learning from them to improve her future.

Her parents and brother also seemed to resent Sidonie for not having made some of the same major mistakes they had, such as physical and/or psychological abuse, infidelity, drug abuse, having their children in inappropriate environments, having predators in their children's lives, etc. They should have been proud of Sidonie, but they wanted her to be down to their level and continued to attempt to place her there. Her husband received some of these abuses and behaviors only because he was married to Sidonie. That was not fair to him and she felt as though she had done wrong by bringing him into that, although she had tried to warn him before he married her. It was not as bad for him though and he believed her worth it. Sidonie was their main target and received the worst when her husband was not present. As within her childhood, it was always when others were not present.

Sidonie is a problem solver. She focuses on solutions, not the problem. She spent those years attempting everything she could think of, then reanalyzing in hopes of thinking of more to attempt in her efforts to establish and maintain good relationships with her parents and brother. Nothing she attempted worked. They would never make the effort to do their part to overcome their issues or quit projecting them onto Sidonie to have better relationships with her. They would not even acknowledge to themselves that they had issues. Her mom had gradually convinced her father to perceive Sidonie as she did. With both her parents and her brother regularly treating her in such a manner, Sidonie could no longer have them actively involved in her life. She had the courage to attempt to change her relationships with each of them for the better, then she gained the wisdom to know that she could not, so she developed the serenity to accept them for the way they are. She has learned that acceptance is very powerful with matters that cannot be changed. That has benefited her in many situations throughout her adult life.

Sidonie was fortunate to have had the opportunities to learn from others what family dynamics should be. She had spent much time with a couple of friends and their families while growing up. It was from those families that she learned physical and psychological abuse in the home was not normal and should not occur. It was also from those parents and other parents as she grew into an adult that she learned the true role of a father and the true role of a mother. She witnessed the difference in their relationships with their children. She had never had that. Sidonie had to accept that her mom would never be a mom to her in the true sense of that role. That was very difficult to accept. Many times, she has needed such a mom, but has never had that. Her mom will not allow Sidonie to have a relationship with her dad without being the center of that relationship controlling and limiting it.

Her brother and she had been very close during their early childhood. In many ways he was a brother in the true sense of that role until he changed toward her for popularity. It was a permanent change, even after he lost that popularity in the dysfunction of his own issues. Sidonie had to accept that he would never again be such a brother to her. Realizing her immediate family's lack of self-awareness in their own behaviors helped Sidonie forgive them all again and move on.

She first stopped interacting with her brother. When they were both with family at the same time, Sidonie attempted to avoid him. She kept any interaction between them very brief and blunt. Then, she was finally able to convince her husband to move away. She had been wanting to move from that area since early in their marriage, but her husband was never willing to leave his family in addition to everyone and everything he knew, until he realized that her parents' interference in their life was negatively affecting Sidonie, their children, and their life together. Constantly dealing with their negativity caused Sidonie to become negative. She attempted to limit their knowledge of her and her life, which included her husband and children, as much as possible to avoid dealing with their ridicule of everything she did and their attempts at control of their decisions with harsh criticisms. That move away from her parents intensified their behavior toward her which significantly affected her children, so she did not interact with her parents for an entire year.

That was many years ago. Sidonie has since kept her parents' involvement in her life very limited, and she still does not have a relationship with her brother. It is never easy to exclude family from one's life. She has needed them but knew they could never be there for her the way she needed. She does feel somewhat like an orphan, but that is much better than the alternative. Her mom has always made difficult situations worse when Sidonie needed her to make them better. The abuse from them has ceased as they do not have the opportunity. She maintained all the progress she had made within herself those many years ago. Despite their efforts, her family was not able to send her back to that cold, dark, desolate place in which she hated herself and believed herself unworthy.

Many of Sidonie's family members dislike the mention of past abuse in any home. They believe it should never be mentioned as if it never occurred and should be forgotten. They think that anyone who mentions it does so because they are still struggling with it and allowing it to affect their lives. Sidonie perceives that past abuse as lessons. Her dad is no longer that very angry man inflicting abuse on others. The lessons from that abuse can be helpful to others. There are many lessons to be learned, such as how not to treat people and what treatment to not allow of oneself, how to remove oneself from such abuse or environments of abuse, and how to deal with and overcome the damage from that abuse. Her dad could share his regrets and how he learned to stop abusing. No one wants to make the abusers feel bad about the past abuse they inflicted when it is no longer occurring, but they should have dealt with the consequences of their abusiveness and overcome it. Perhaps all those who believe it should not be mentioned are the ones who are still struggling with it. Perhaps the mention of it still hurts them and brings many buried issues that still exist to the surface.

Chapter 5

Sidonie was born into a very dysfunctional family. She was raised with their demented ideals and examples and their lack of morales, values, and knowledge. She never had the true innocence of a child. She had always known of the bad and evil of the world. She knew disturbing truths of life that many did not. She has imagined how peaceful and free it must have been for those children who did not always have to live in survival mode in a jungle of predators and abusers. She knows adults who are still shocked by such atrocities done to others which she either experienced or witnessed as a very young child. She is sometimes somewhat envious, not necessarily of them, but of the innocent childhood they were allowed to have.

She suffered much abuse directly and indirectly,

becoming dysfunctional herself. Through it all, Sidonie maintained her values, morales, and some self-respect. She stayed true to herself and never conformed to society. She only wanted to be seen beyond her insecurities of herself, which had been instilled in her, for who she truly was, not an image. She paved her own path while struggling to deal with everything she had experienced and witnessed. Amazingly, she never self-destructed. That within itself triumphed all odds against her. Most people who experience only a fraction of what Sidonie experienced self-destruct in some significant, life-altering way. She somehow had the wisdom she needed to deal with it all in a healthier manner without guilt or major regrets. Professional help was not an option for Sidonie as she could not afford it. However, she has been grateful for having done it on her own with the help of those who boosted her self-esteem with their respect and appreciation for who she was. Her gratefulness is for those people and the magnitude of wisdom, understanding, and knowledge she acquired about people, life, and herself.

Sidonie has heard many adults express their desire to return to their childhood as it was much easier without adult responsibilities. She has never wanted to return to any part of her childhood. She does not believe she would survive it a second time. Sidonie is still very confident that moving from her parent's home when she did was the best decision she ever made for herself personally. That was the main step toward recovery and becoming the functional person she became.

Sidonie has been a confidante of many people of all social statuses who grew up in and are living all types of lifestyles who have shared with her their difficult and traumatizing experiences. She is not any less than anyone because such things happen to people of all statuses, not only low ones as she had felt she was in for a long time. She learned that because people are different, they are affected differently by the same things. Therefore, they deal with things differently, but each one is special, amazing, and awesome in each their own way, and each person can overcome to find their way in life.

She has also learned that the abuse within her family is considered to be a cycle because the abuse is passed down through generations. Sidonie has been told, by those who were aware of at least some of the abuse, that she has broken that cycle with herself which is evident with the family she created. She broke two cycles, one of her paternal family and one of her maternal family. The family cycle of her paternal family did not only continue within her immediate family but that of some of her individual extended families as well. She did not realize at the time that she was breaking the family cycle of abuse. She was simply determined not to treat her own family or anyone else like that of the family she was born into. She was also determined to not allow herself to be treated like that in her home, nor allow her children to be in environments where such behaviors occurred. Sidonie refused for her children to experience that trauma or have those examples. She had rarely and only in her moments of most intense hatred for herself projected her issues onto others in her teen and very early adult years. As she grew older and became aware of that concept, she chose to be consciencely mindful not to do so. If she had not, she would have likely continued that cycle of abuse as her life became hectic with more responsibilities and pressures and sometimes very overwhelming. She believes that dealing with, overcoming, and healing from the abuse is how she was able to break the cycle because she no longer had those negative feelings to project onto others as her parents and brother continued to do, nor as other family members did, and her grandfather had.

Sidonie had wondered if her molesters had been affected by their actions, impairing their lives somehow or if the young boy was able to make peace with it as she did. The older girl should have understood well enough to know better at her age. Sidonie decided she had to let go of that girl's choice to do what she did to Sidonie for her own healing. You could say she forgave her, but it was more the realization of something profound. The best revenge was to flourish, not allowing her abuser to impair her life. Sidonie believed that her life would ultimately be better than that girl's because Sidonie would overcome it and move on without it impairing her future, while that girl would have to live with that horrible wrong she did for the rest of her life. That girl would remember what she did to that young child while she was raising her own children. Sidonie was no longer that child and no longer had to suffer that trauma nor did she have to suffer any guilt because she was not the perpetrator. She realized that flourishing far beyond that which the girl ever would, would somehow release Sidonie from the control the girl had over her through the damage she had done to Sidonie. Flourishing would repair the damage. She applied the same to her other perpetrators of her adult life. She proved to be correct. She was released as she flourished.

Without retrieving those childhood memories which had been blocked, Sidonie would not have been able to overcome the issues they had created, nor would she have been able to heal from the trauma. It was a two year emotionally brutal journey resulting in complete freedom from the heavy burden of it all and beautiful healing. She left a deep, dark, lonely place and entered an endless space of light and freedom. She felt as though she could finally breathe deeply and freely for the first time.

As Sidonie was dealing with her childhood trauma, she had new damaging and traumatizing situations arise. Each of those situations set her back in her progress of dealing and healing. As she took two steps forward, she was pushed back a step. Sometimes it was one step forward then two steps back. Those incidents retracted what little progress she had made with improving her self-esteem and self-worth. Then, she was back to where she had begun, feeling not good enough in addition to all the other negative feelings she had about herself in all those prior years.

The one thing Sidonie never did was give up. Sometimes she wanted to, but she could not because she could not remain in that dark place with those negative, painful emotions. She had known many people who used drugs to cope with their traumas. Her brother was one. They chose temporary relief from the pain instead of dealing with it directly for permanent resolution. Sidonie wanted permanent resolution. She knew she would not get that through drugs. She later realized she probably would have become an addict as some, such as her brother, had she made that choice. Her brother's addiction was brief, but his issues remain. Sidonie always continued moving forward, even when she did not think she could. She did it to get through her situations quicker and beyond the emotional pain sooner. She believes that was the best way for her because it was productive. She moved passed the events and progressed, learning from each experience to better and more easily navigate through life. She has peace now and life is good with the family she has created.

Sidonie's final moment of recovery was when she realized that she triumphed. She triumphed over everyone who had ever attempted to inhibit her by setting her back, holding her back, and knocking her down. She triumphed by overcoming it all and flourishing. She has sympathy for those who have not overcome their issues and continue to struggle through life. Sidonie did not make mistakes that permanently affected her life negatively or with guilt and serious regrets, however, she knows that she could have still overcome such mistakes. One's course can always be changed if needed. Sidonie understands the huge accomplishment of overcoming traumas and significant mistakes as well as the importance of being proud of oneself for such accomplishment. She recognizes the importance of focusing more on accomplishments than failures and judging oneself for who they are today, not when they were struggling and lost.

Focusing on accomplishments is an incentive to have more of them because they make a person feel good about themselves, but it is important to not forget the lessons learned from failures. It is also important to hold oneself accountable for their wrongs. Without that self-conviction, people can easily lose their way and accumulate only failures. She wishes others would learn to apply those things to themselves, as well as to others before judging them. Living through impairing situations then flourishing is something to be extremely proud of. Perception is huge in life. It is very beneficial to look for positives in each situation regardless of how bad the situation may be to prevent sinking into a dark place. People can at least gain knowledge and/or wisdom from each situation, even if it is only how to prevent another such situation from occurring.

Sidonie appreciates that nothing significant ever occurred between herself and Chrétien because it would have been a difficult situation considering her history with his brother. He is still in the same place in life as he was all those years ago. He has never progressed and has not built a life for himself. She could not have built a life with him. She had made the correct decisions by being cautious with him. Sidonie is grateful that none of her previous relationships were successful because she would not have found her way to her husband. She now has the relationship, love, and life she wanted and still wants.

With her desire to help others, Sidonie has used her acquired knowledge, wisdom, and understanding to assist others in finding their way. She befriended someone older who was struggling through her life after divorce with three children. Sidonie helped her with encouraging, optimistic perspectives. She gave her hope and motive to continue toward a better future, which she acquired in time. Sidonie also helped younger people who lacked self-esteem and social skills. She befriended them using her outgoing personality and treated them as any person without such issues. She encouraged them and coached them to think differently about themselves and others around them. She brought them out of their timidness and assisted them in building their self-esteem to where they functioned well in life and no longer needed Sidonie. She has listened to many people understanding their struggles and teaching them to be proud of their accomplishments, which they had not recognized as accomplishments. She helped them perceive that they were better people than they had realized and had lived better lives than they had realized. Her perspectives and insights gave value to them, which they had not had until Sidonie valued them.

Sidonie's mom had issues with Sidonie befriending such people. She perceived those people as being beneath them, which was ironic. Those were people struggling with issues from traumas or lack of what they had needed during their childhoods. Sidonie's mom also had issues. Her issues not being as noticeable did not make her any better than those whose issues were obvious. She did not understand what Sidonie was doing and would have never acknowledged Sidonie's ability to do so. Some people will find their way without extra help. Some people will never find their way without assistance from people like Sidonie. Those people Sidonie has helped built good lives and have had happiness. That has fulfilled Sidonie as she knows that she has served a purpose beyond that of the basic duties of life.

Loving oneself is the most impowering of all. It is important to love oneself because each person must live with theirself every second of their life. There is no escape. We would be miserable spending every moment of our lives with someone we did not love. If we are miserable with ourselves, we will also make anyone with us miserable. Loving oneself does not mean being selfish, inconsiderate, or uncompassionate toward others, but we must love ourselves to be able to have healthy, functional relationships. Also, if we love ourselves, we are not desperate to be loved by others. That desperation can result in toxic relationships. The more one loves oneself, the more one can nurture oneself.

Ever since Sidonie could remember, she had knowledge and wisdom which has always guided her. It was like a silent voice inside her informing her what to do and not do, what was right and what was wrong. She witnessed many children grow up living the negative influences they had from their parents and others as though those behaviors were normal but have impaired their lives as adults. She always somehow knew those things were immoral, wrong, and harmful to her development as well as the development of all children. When Sidonie would share her intuition with her mother, she would always tell Sidonie she was wrong. She taught Sidonie to dismiss her intuition. Sidonie realized along the way that she had always felt a spiritual connection. That spiritual connection seemed to weaken some during the time she ignored her intuition. Then, it strengthened as she focused more on the guidance of right and wrong during her confusing teenage years.

She often rebelled against social norms as she was very confident that they were wrong because they went against morals that she thought everyone had. Sidonie chose to not do what most others her age were doing during her teens because she knew the damage the consequences could do to her and her life, including her future near, far, and possibly permanently. She seemed to always have wisdom that others did not. When her pain and loneliness became unbearable, she spoke to and cried to God. When she felt in danger, she clung to Him for protection. When she did not know what decision to make, she asked Him for the answer. He comforted her. He protected her from the worst and more. He provided her answers with total clarity. Even in her loneliest moments, Sidonie knew she was not completely alone. She always had God and he always kept her on track. He provided her with strength and guidance. Her spiritual connection to Him was her lifeline. All her knowledge and wisdom of life was from God as was her intuition.

As she grew older, Sidonie's spiritual connection grew even stronger. Sidonie has pondered why many people she has known self-destructed with negative behaviors impairing them more and taking them longer to find their way, and why some have still not been able to find their way. She always had a silent voice inside guiding her of right and wrong, harmful and beneficial, destructive and constructive. Perhaps others simply ignored that guidance or had it blocked somehow. She may never understand why she was different from so many in this regard.

Overcoming all the trauma allowed Sidonie to

become fully functional in life and flourish. During that process, she acquired a great understanding of people, how situations affect them, and how their issues are transferred to others. This has enabled her to learn to escape any continued attempts of abuse and not be traumatized by any of it. She has gained much wisdom and has continued to gain more from each difficult challenge in life. She has learned much and acquired new tools with each challenge to use for the next. Ultimately, life is about love. Sidonie loves herself first, then loves all others from whatever distance she is capable of.

www.ingramcontent.com/pod-product-compliance
Lightning Source LLC
LaVergne TN
LVHW091324150826
845673LV00006B/1763

* 9 7 9 8 8 9 3 8 3 3 0 1 0 *